Innovative Management Using Telecommunications

Innovative Management Using Telecommunications

A GUIDE TO OPPORTUNITIES, STRATEGIES, AND APPLICATIONS

HERBERT S. DORDICK

Temple University

FREDERICK WILLIAMS

The University of Texas

JOHN WILEY & SONS
New York / Chichester / Brisbane / Toronto / Singapore

Library of Congress Cataloging-in-Publication Data:

Dordick, Herbert S., 1925–
  Innovative Management Using Telecommunications

  Bibliography: p.
  Includes index.
  1. Industrial management—Communication systems.
2. Telecommunication. 3. Telephone in business.
4. Office practice—Automation. I. Williams, Frederick,
1933– . II. Title.

HF5541.T4D67 1986   658.4'5   86-7797
ISBN 0-471-81296-X
Printed in the United States of America
10 9 8 7 6 5 4 3 2 1

*To the memory of Ithiel de Sola Pool,
scholar and friend, who would be pleased with this marriage
of theory to the practical.*

Preface

Like our earlier well-received *The Executive's Guide to Information Technology*, we've written this book for busy executives who want to profit from the revolution in office technologies but are more interested in gaining a competitive edge than in mastering technical details. This book concentrates on the latest telecommunications devices and systems that range from the new breed of "intelligent" telephones to the cost savings and managerial advantages of having your own "local area network." However, this is more than an executive tour of these technologies; you'll meet a fascinating range of new opportunities for banking, research, communications, holding meetings, communications–transportation tradeoffs, marketing, and training. You'll see how the executive's world is changing before your very eyes and how the right choices of telecommunications will put you ahead of your competition.

We have written in the practical, business oriented language of the manager rather than the technician. Most of the advice in this book has come directly from our research, consulting, and teaching experiences in telecommunications management. We know that it works and that it will work for you.

HERBERT S. DORDICK
FREDERICK WILLIAMS

Philadelphia, Pennsylvania
Austin, Texas
July 1986

Contents

Innovative
Management Using
Telecommunications

PART ONE

NEW OPPORTUNITIES FOR INNOVATIVE EXECUTIVES

1

PUT THE TELECOMMUNICATIONS REVOLUTION TO WORK FOR YOU

BAD NEWS . . . GOOD NEWS

Last year, Phil was going around in circles trying to open the new midwest office of his rapidly growing industrial real estate firm. As Phil heard it from his office manager, who was supposed to get everything in order for the new office, the hassle was in getting the specialized communications services the office needed to maintain contact with both the select list of client-investors and the home office. He had read about the new "telecommunications" and his office manager gave him even more to read about discount long distance services, mobile phones, fax, and "intelligent" telephones. His office manager reported that things had become more complicated than just plain old telephone services. There were so many new options, like dealing with three different companies—one for equipment, another for local services, and yet another for long distance—and one-stop telephone service. Telecommunications had become too important to his business to leave it up to his office manager. He would just have to jump in and learn about it for himself. And he did.

Things are now looking up; Phil discovered numerous advantages when he took the time to look into his new telecommunications options. For one, he is benefiting from the tax advantages of owning his own phone equipment. He found that his telephone and his switchboard, a computerlike desktop piece of equipment, was really intelligent—from auto-dialing to a top rate intercom system. Espe-

3

cially important for his communications intensive business, Phil has cut his long distance costs by 20 percent. Now he is looking into the electronic mail and the "fax" services he has been reading about. He has discovered too, that he might be able to talk, send, and receive data or facsimile on his system without having to add new wires and switchboards. All of this is a real winner for his real estate business. In fact he has already begun to think about new services he can offer his clients.

Phil's story is not unique in this era of deregulation and divestiture coupled with space-age advances in telecommunications and computing. The bad news has been that we have all had to pay more attention to our equipment and service options and have often had to suffer from delays and confusion while the new telecommunications business goes through its growing pains. But the good news can be cost savings, time savings, and even opportunities for new businesses.

None of the good news comes easily, however. Like everything else in business, it requires effective planning and management. You must know your needs and what resources can be made available to best meet them. This is no small order in today's "information age." New technologically based options are around nearly every corner, many opening up new opportunities for managerial innovations. The new telecommunications can put cash flow data at your fingertips any time of the day or night. "What if?" financial projections no longer require a two-day turnaround from your data processing department; you can do them on your desktop computer on Sunday evening if you wish and get immediate results. Your managerial team can be in instantaneous touch; teleconferencing substitutes information movement for people movement.

The new technologies are changing managerial roles. The "organization person" of the industrial era is being replaced by the new entrepreneurs of the information age. How you do business and even the types of business you do are in a period of visible change. In fact the success or failure of your business, if not its competitive edge, may well be a direct result of how well you plan and manage the new telecommunications.

As Phil summed it up:

Managing my telecommunications problems has not only improved the way I do business, but has opened up new businesses to do. I've become a better manager.

MANAGEMENT AS AN INFORMATION-INTENSIVE ACTIVITY

Information Businesses versus Information in Businesses

Much of the popular literature about the so-called information age stresses the growth of businesses that deal directly with information. Phil's real estate business fits partly in that category as information about property availability, investor–clients, and money markets is crucial to his success. But some businesses deal directly with information as their primary product, as, for example, a research and development organization, a consulting service, an investment firm, or the traditional newspaper or broadcasting station. The primary output of a telephone common carrier, your telephone company, is the transfer of information, and this is the information business. Even many types of computing services are essentially information businesses.

Although these businesses are on the growth curve of our times, they represent a relatively small percentage, perhaps slightly more than 10 percent, of the nation's output. As businesses, they do not represent the real power of information. Instead, we should think of information as a resource that is critical to the efficient management of today's organizations, critical to organizational productivity, and in many cases proves to be a source of new products, services, and industries.

The growth of information-intensive management has been in both internal and external spheres of operation. Internally, we have seen the explosion of clerical activities that represent the daily operation of many organizations—including record-keeping, routine correspondence, ordering, invoicing, and handling inquiries. The managerial challenge is to make these information-handling activities efficient, a task that itself involves an information-intensive interaction between labor and management. There is also the internal information involved in the monitoring and controlling of product or service flow, for example, as in manufacturing control, inventory maintenance, and shipping. Externally, there is the need to gather and interpret market (or client) data, to know the status of supplies, to communicate a public image, and to be able to draw on the money market.

In the largest view of information-intensive management—a concept that is developed further in Chapter 3—the basic success, if not survival, of a business depends on the ability of management

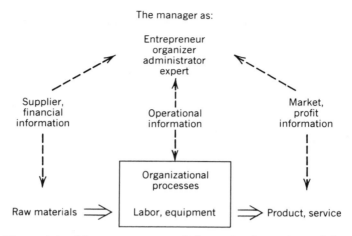

Figure 1.1.   Management as an information-intensive activity

to understand the relation between what the market will support and the value that the organization can add to its resources of labor, management, and raw material. As summarized in Figure 1.1, this is a view of management as an information-intensive activity. Or in the case of government, public schools, or nonprofit institutions, what services can be efficiently generated and equitably distributed to meet the demands of the society?

Information in Management

That information is a factor in management is not a new idea, but the growth of its criticality is. Increasingly, the capability to obtain, interpret, and disseminate information can make the difference between success and failure in modern management. Three factors underlie the growth of the information component. First, as organizations have grown in size and complexity (e.g., multinationals and conglomerates), there is a corresponding growth in the magnitude of information activities necessary for management. As an organization grows, so does its "information overhead," sometimes exponentially. Second, managerial skills have increasingly taken advantage of information for the improvement of organizational effectiveness. The importance of research and development, the science of management and of manufacturing control, or modern techniques of market research are examples. Indeed, in many modern businesses, the ability to employ information-intensive managerial techniques may provide the competitive edge. Third, the growth of computing and telecommunications technologies in the information age is allowing us to amplify our human information-handling capabilities much as the industrial age was launched when the machine expanded our capacity for labor.

Modern telecommunications, both in itself and as it distributes the power of computing, is contributing visibly to the growth of the information component in management. In the broad view, there are four areas of impact: (1) the automation and semiautomation of clerical work, (2) expansion of the span of managerial capability, (3) changes in the way you do business, and (4) changes in the business you do.

FOUR IMPACTS ON MODERN MANAGERS

The Automation or Semiautomation of Clerical Work

Technologies such as computerized accounting systems, word processing, and database management have provided for the automation or semiautomation of many aspects of clerical work. Although many of these innovations are more directly attributable to the implementation of computers than telecommunications, the mark of the modern organization is that these two technologies are implemented as powerful combinations.

The automated teller machine is one of the major success stories of clerical automation. Not only has labor been largely automated by the technology, but the small amount of labor that remains is contributed by the customer rather than the bank employee. (Watch next for banks to get you to do your transactions directly via desktop terminals in your office or home. Their cost of processing an electronic check is about one-fifth that of a traditional paper one.)

Although these advances increase the need for capital investment in information technology and telecommunications systems and services, they reduce the need for labor and its supervision. Data entry tasks, summary report preparation, and distribution are largely automated with important status information continuously available via the telecommunications network.

Expansion of Your Managerial Span

Recently one of America's top 10 organizations proudly announced that they had eliminated an entire echelon of middle-level managers in their executive ranks. Another way they described their feat was that they had essentially doubled the number of employees that any one manager could effectively supervise.

As automation of clerical activities proceeds, there is less need for immediate supervision. The standardization of work is either embedded in the software of the system (as in a word processor or PBX) or the software can guide the clerical worker through less routine operations, in effect acting as supervisor. Many new office systems can provide performance data on clerical operations, and these data can be conveyed directly to higher level supervisors, lessening the need for intermediaries.

Even more dramatic changes are in the expansion of the manager's span of activities. Access to remote databases increases the amount of information available for decision-making. Organizational communication systems allow for the direct exchange of information among a far wider number of employees than heretofore possible. The capability for extra-office communication networks makes it possible for the managerial grid to easily extend among branches of a company to satellite work centers, or even to workers in the home.

The increased intelligence of modern telecommunications networks made possible by the introduction of computer technology as an integral part of these networks is significantly altering the nature of management. Opening and freeing the traditional patterns of information flow from the constraints of time and space has resulted in what may be called a managerial revolution. Intelligent networks can free managers to manage. Consequently, there is a flattening of the managerial pyramid.

Changes in the Way You Do Business

It is a restricted view to consider only how information technologies can improve an existing way of doing business. In fact, a major source of failure in implementing information technologies is to fix in place what is already an inefficient operation. For example, there are endless anecdotes about how computers have been installed to automate complex record systems (hospitals are notorious for this), only to determine later that a large share of the records was traditionally unutilized. The successful scenario is to thoroughly evaluate the existing system, then modify or replace it before installing the new information technology.

Consider the example of a firm with a large staff of marketing representatives that installed an intelligent telephone system to improve communications with their salespersons in the field. However, they soon found that the telephone system they had purchased made it very easy and inexpensive to deal directly with many of their customers using today's telemarketing techniques (see Chapter 16). Technology enabled them not merely to enhance an existing way of doing business but to *change the way they did business*.

Changes in the Business You Do

The changing business of a microcomputer software distributor offers an example of this opportunity. This urban based firm entered into the software business early when the proliferation of manufacturers made it increasingly difficult for retailers to maintain liaison (and lines of credit) with a wide variety of companies, the list of which changed weekly. By the mid-1980s, the distribution business began to suffer as many manufacturers were shaken out of the market and retailers began to deal directly with the most successful of the survivors. Yet the distributor, to his surprise, found business growing in another direction. As a special benefit to retailers as well as their customers, the distributor had developed an effective "help line" (800 number call-in) to answer questions regarding major products. This activity had also branched to several large corporations who had contracted with the distributor not only for longer-range help line service but on-site training as well. Today, this company is primarily in the software installation and training business, although it still maintains its wholesale operations. Telecommunications technology opened a new business opportunity for this distributor. There is, most likely, yet another mode of distributing software on the horizon. Essentially, software is information and it can be distributed via the telecommunications network, in effect "downloading" the software package to the subscriber of the service.

Telecommunications makes possible businesses and products that heretofore were not possible. Bear in mind that *USA Today* significantly changed the nature of the newspaper business and the Merrill Lynch Cash Management Accounts introduced a new way of managing one's money.

Another example comes from the developer of shopping centers.

For many years, this individual capitalized on talents in land acquisition and facilities planning. Recently, however, telecommunications deregulation has made it attractive for the company to integrate telecommunications services (e.g., telephone, data, security) into the packages it offers its lessors. In effect, the developer has also gone into the telecommunications business.

The changing information environment, including deregulation, the marketplace, and your ability to create new sources of revenue by the implementation of information technologies not only changes the way you can do business, but the business you do.

WHERE ARE YOU IN THE REVOLUTION?

You can gauge your position by taking a brief tour of the most visible of the modern telecommunications technologies and applications as summarized in Chapter 2. Then you can consider how they will improve the operation of your organization.

But, as in Chapter 3, it is not the technologies themselves that contribute to your business or organization. It is in how they can make you and your staff more valuable in the work that you do. This is your challenge as a manager. You must seek to capitalize on the information revolution to improve human capabilities.

If you are not now responding to that challenge, remember that your competition may get there first.

2
AN EXECUTIVE TOUR OF THE NEW TELECOMMUNICATIONS

WHAT ARE THE NEW TELECOMMUNICATIONS?

Forces Shaping the Future

Three forces are shaping the modern telecommunications environment. First, we are witnessing many of the benefits brought about by extraordinarily rapid advancements in microelectronics. The multitalented semiconductor chips have come down from space and into the office.

Second, technical developments have integrated computing and communicating. So much of our new telephone equipment incorporates computer power that it is difficult to know where one leaves off and the other begins. Examine one of the new desktop electronic switchboards or PBXs (Private Branch Exchanges) and you will see rows of semiconductor chips doing the switching. Or if you have a personal computer, perhaps you have already discovered how easily you can transmit data over plain old telephone lines. The convergence of telecommunications and computing has restructured the telecommunications equipment and systems market. In fact, computer manufacturers and telecommunications manufacturers see their futures in each other's markets. A new and leaner AT&T is aggressively pursuing the computer business. Developments in telecommunications that are so important to managers are also computer developments.

11

Third, we are visibly moving toward an economy highly sensitive to the flow of information. As introduced in Chapter 1, this is the "age" where information can not only give you a competitive edge in manufacturing, services, and management, but where it is also becoming a commodity itself to be produced and marketed. The latest and best information is necessary to know what to sell where, or how to manufacture the latest design that will attract customers. The information technologies are increasingly the basis of our manufacturing and control systems. Few modern managers would be able to fulfill their responsibilities without exercising effective control over their information resources, and to do so they must manage and control their telecommunications.

New Technologies for Managing Better

The most visible of telecommunications technologies represent the strong supply-side emphasis in bringing you everything from new telephone systems to the promise of your own private telecommunications networks. Table 2.1 summarizes the highlights of seven such technologies that are competing for their place in the modern management environment.

Note how the technologies in Table 2.1 often represent combinations of telecommunications and computing. "Intelligent" chips facilitate the operation of the telecommunications network and send-receive equipment; the network itself distributes the power of computing. Taken together, these technologies provide for a multitude of new services and applications, or in the larger sense, new opportunities for the innovative executive.

Table 2.1. High Visibility Telecommunications Technologies

Telecommunications Technology	What It Does	How It Helps You Manage
Intelligent phones	Microprocessor (computer) based capabilities that provide the convenience services such as autodialing, redialing, call forwarding, call waiting, call transfer, or conference calling.	Saves you time and travel, cuts down telephone-tag, saves clerical time and anxiety of missing the client or sale.
Voice-data PBXs (switchboards)	Today's switchboard; the computer has made it the "brain" of your office; fully automatic and programmable for call routing, controlling toll call access, and optimal routing of calls to save time and money; sets call priorities, keeps call records, and is the gateway to other networks.	No operator! Cut telecom costs according to your priorities and arrange your communication needs to suit your management style. Change the system easily and efficiently as your needs change.
Long distance networks	Satellites, optical fiber, cable, new microwave networks, and deregulation have expanded new transmission options for voice and data.	Significant cost savings for specialized networks dedicated to meet your personal and firm's management needs. Improves coordination and control.
Personal computer communications	"Full feature" personal computers, including lap-size portables and hand-held communications versions, allow for computing and communications well beyond the confines of the office. New advances include networks linked by hand-held send-and-receive terminals linked by radio.	Managers can manage, plan, keep in touch, control, hire and fire, and coordinate from anywhere.

Table 2.1. (Continued)

Telecommunications Technology	What It Does	How It Helps You Manage
Local area networks	A privately installed network for computer communications use from office automation to systems for manufacturing control. Some systems may provide for voice as well as data communications at various speeds. Digital Termination Services, Cellular Mobile, and others are often used for a local area network.	Provides management with complete control of local communications, for security and reliability over data resources. Expands administrative span of control.
Mobile phones and paging	Cellular radio technology increases the number of mobile channels or phone lines hundredfold and reduces waiting times and busy signals or blocking. Telephone calls from autos, trains, and even airplanes.	Maintain contact with your staff while driving or flying, even from places where there are no wired telephones. You can also use cellular mobile as a telephone radio bypass between your branch offices.
	Paging includes the traditional beeper to tell someone to place a call and new technologies that transmit short messages to a small alphanumeric receiver.	Provides instant personal access to key staff, especially in emergencies. You remain in control.
Facsimile	High speed digital networks allow for the transmission of large documents, including visuals.	Transmit reports, blueprints, illustrated product catalogs almost instantaneously. Increases and enriches your information base with visuals at lower cost than video.

New Services and Applications

On the other side of the distinction between technologies themselves and their broader applications are what we've increasingly come to call the "teleservices." As summarized in Table 2.2, some of the names of these services are now generic—as with "teleconferencing" or "telemarketing"—while others are terms to which we have chosen to affix the "tele" prefix.

These services represent changes in the managerial environment—literally new alternatives in time and space. Many of these services provide for the substitution of communication for transportation. Teleconferencing makes meetings possible by bringing participants together electronically rather than by physical presence. Computer-based conferencing frees participants from the restrictions of time and space. Similarly, telecommuting substitutes work movement for people movement, and telemailing trades electronic message movement for paper movement. The benefits are increased flexibility, cost-cutting, and new opportunities for extending the span of managerial control.

Table 2.2. The New "Teleservices"

Telecommunications Service or Application	What It Does	Management Implications
Telebanking	A form of electronic mail but designed for financial transactions. Transfers "electronic money." Provides instant access to balances.	Instant cash management allows you to keep track of your financial resources, and make certain you are getting the best use of your cash. Allows you to "make money with money."
Teleresearching (databases)	Commercial databases now offer information ranging from market prices to news headlines. These are easily accessed by computers, including PCs. Some include mail services. Other utilities represent developing forms of "electronic publishing," the "Videotex" you hear about.	Provides the information you need for decision making and planning. Immediate access to latest information for market research. Information you develop on the job may be new products for you to market on the information utility.

Table 2.2. (Continued)

Telecommunications Service or Application	What It Does	Management Implications
Telemailing	Mail sent by various telecommunications forms, including computer to computer, computer to post office, computer to courier for delivery, as well as facsimile transmission methods.	Eliminates telephone tag, provides "instant" delivery bypassing office bottlenecks. Easy and reliable but has certain acknowledgment routines. Word processors can be originators and receivers of electronic mail.
Teleconferencing	Provides for group communication by linking participants via voice, text, or video communications.	Allows the manager to be in many places at the same time; reduces time away from office yet links your widely separated staff. Makes routine meetings more efficient and encourages "silent" staff to participate. Reduces costs of coordination.
Telecommuting	Use the telecommunications network to transport your work to wherever you are instead of transporting yourself to the office. Decentralize clerical work by satellite offices or "work at home" programs.	Manage whenever or wherever you wish; be free of the office. Recruit work forces independent of high priced transportation or downtown parking. Use part-time workers in their homes. But you will have to learn how to manage workers who are not in your workspace.
Telemarketing	Use inbound or outbound telephone lines for direct sales as well as keeping in close contact with your customers. Use "800" numbers or discount rates for inexpensive services. Substitute for direct sales calls.	The fastest growing area of marketing can cut your costs of customer contact by a ratio of more than 10 to 1. Also offers excellent opportunities for marketing tie-in with direct mail and/or broadcast advertising. Can be very flexible for bringing new products to market in a matter of days.

16

Table 2.2. (Continued)

Telecommunications Service or Application	What It Does	Management Implications
Teletraining	Use new online services for training or help with new technologies. Take short courses or university seminars via telecommunications links.	Not only training but the innovative delivery of it is a key to success with modern telecommunications and services. Allows for training on the job site rather than in expensive classes.

YOUR USES OF TELECOMMUNICATIONS

What Do You Manage?

Ask yourself: What is unique about what you manage? How can the new telecommunications affect what you do?

In a large organization, your efforts may be concentrated on one or two managerial tasks. For example, if you are a personnel officer, you may be much more engaged in daily administration than, say, if you were a marketing manager where your contributions might concentrate on planning. Or if your responsibilities are to keep a production line efficient, you might spend the bulk of your time in evaluation. Perhaps you are managing in a creative or artistic environment where your job takes on the special challenges of motivating creative personnel. This could be the antithesis of managing an engineering staff where schedules, costs, and deadlines are readily accepted facts of life. Or consider managing in a hospital or a university where many of the decisions are often made by the professionals and the manager's primary role may be to coordinate and implement these decisions.

In smaller organizations, you may perform a wide range of tasks, for example, as the manager of a retail store, a small real estate company, a modest size brokerage or consulting firm, or a five-person manufacturing shop. You may carry the responsibilities for everything from planning to evaluation, not excluding the role of a general troubleshooter. Often your challenge will be not to become so preoccupied with one or several of these tasks that you overlook the others.

Table 2.3. Information Activities of Managerial Roles

Information Activities of the Manager as:

Entrepreneur

Gathers information about economic, political, and social environments in order to explore new growth opportunities. Evaluates alternative opportunities for business expansion. Formulates corporate goals and objectives and communicates these to staff, to financial community, and to the market. Formulates strategic plans and develops policies for achieving them. Oversees the development of operating plans.

Organizer

Keeps staff informed of corporate goals and activities. Takes the lead in promoting new ideas and making changes necessary to advance business goals. Builds and maintains employee morale and teamwork. Represents firm to the world by way of correspondence, advertising, and public appearances.

Administrator

Schedules and coordinates activities; verifies that tasks have been performed. Maintains communications with staff at all times. Maintains communications with clients and information providers at all times and from all places.

Expert

Must be aware of sources of information important to the business and must develop means for accessing these sources. Must be capable of creating useful information from vast quantities of data. The manager as expert listens to and queries staff members, colleagues, and competitors for information relevant to the business. Corresponds with sources of information via the mail and telephone. Attends information seeking and gathering meetings. Exchanges information with colleagues and staff. Employs consultants to learn more and to verify information gathered. Selects and stores information for later use.

Across the differences in environment and special demands, there are four basic roles typically expected of you as a manager. You are expected to be an entrepreneur, an organizer, an administrator, and an expert. Each of these roles is now being changed by the telecommunications and computing revolution. Table 2.3 summarizes these roles in considering management as an information-intensive activity.

Your Role as Entrepreneur

What are your managerial goals? Today's business environment is a rapidly changing one and you must use critical judgment to recognize the need to change goals or to alter strategies and plans. You must take risks and anticipate the consequences of failure as well as success. You must plan creatively and with a sense of entrepreneurship. You must always ask the difficult question of "just what is my business?"

Telecommunications and computing advances now place a nearly unlimited variety of information services at your fingertips. For group or collective planning, teleconferencing and dedicated voice and data links make many routine forms of travel unnecessary. The members of your planning group are as close as their communications terminals.

Your Role as Organizer

How will the goals be reached? You must organize the team to be managed, set the schedules and the operational objectives. The aim is to ensure the optimal plan for success.

Simulation and "what if" analyses can aid in maximizing operational planning, which in turn can be disseminated in the telecommunications network. Electronic mail or facsimile services allow rapid dissemination of mixes of data, text, and graphics to your team. The network allows you to stay in close touch.

Your Role as Administrator

Is the daily operation in order? You must implement the schedule, coordinate, and monitor the team effort. Is the organization working as it is supposed to work? What adjustments are necessary? How are breakdowns accommodated? To be effective, you must provide leadership and set examples. An efficient team knows the goals and strategies of the operation and ultimately should be able to perform without you.

Telecommunications extends your span of authority to the limits of the network. Paging and mobile telephone services as well as electronic mail allow instant communication among personnel, and reduced "telephone tag." Daily reports of operations can be automatically evaluated against standards and variance criteria. In-house databases, local area networks, allow instant access to all company records, including daily cash flow via online banking services.

Your Role as Expert

Are goals being met with optimum efficiency? You are constantly challenged to improve the operation, to influence new goal-setting, and ultimately to capitalize on evaluation as a basis for planning.

Operational results can be entered directly into automated planning models, thus completing the managerial cycle. Simulation and "what if" analyses can be employed to evaluate results and compare alternative plans. You can communicate changes in plans instantly to all personnel on the network.

FROM THE BIG BOARD TO MOZART: A DAY IN YOUR LIFE

There is a collective effect to the impact of the new information technologies. They are changing the nature of our daily lives, including the broad pattern of our professional as well as personal endeavors. Here is a possible sample day that you might well experience in the years to come. Obviously not all of these twists will appeal to you, but together they reflect how telecommunications is changing our traditional concepts of time and space—changing how we work (and sometimes play). Further, it shows how telecommunications enables you to play all of the managerial roles.

Your morning begins before breakfast with a quick scan of the messages your computer has gathered for you. First, a brief summary of your key investments—your morning glimpse at how the market closed yesterday. As you scan a brief list of onscreen messages, your eye catches a puzzling note from one of your sales reps in Boston. He reports that a sure sale seems to have gone awry because of the stiff price of some new equipment. You remember the deal but wonder if the quoted price is in line. Because Boston is three hours ahead and it is almost lunchtime there, you decide to tackle the problem now.

While the eggs are boiling, a couple of minutes on your personal computer logs you into the company database where you discover that the deal might be sweetened by a small design change. You send this suggestion to your sales rep with a copy to the design engineer on the project. You log off and sit down to breakfast not too disturbed by this early interruption because it will save you a bevy of phone calls later in the day, and possibly the deal.

Once on the freeway you use your cellular radio phone to call the engineer to make certain she is checking on the design change. You also call your secretary and reschedule several morning appointments so you can follow up on the revised quote.

By the time you reach the office, the engineer has cleared the design change and her assistant has worked up a spreadsheet cost analysis. Materials costs are doublechecked on the company mainframe computer from the same computer terminal running the spreadsheet. You note that your decisions have moved so fast that you can reconfirm the price change with your sales rep prior to his meeting, and to add an extra touch you send a facsimile proposal of the design change, drawings and all, to his client. It will arrive within the hour.

Next you turn to the day's schedule. There is a marketing meeting this morning, lunch with a prospective new hire, a meeting with the research project leader later in the afternoon, and a quick trip to the bank to discuss some financial matters. A busy day, even after having canceled some of the meetings formerly scheduled for the morning.

But not everything is on schedule. A key consultant was snowed in last night in Toronto so she'll miss your important 10:30 A.M. marketing meeting. Your quick-thinking secretary has already suggested that the consultant teleconference with you, so your marketing expert is ready to get on the line if you wish. As this will be better than no meeting at all, you decide to proceed with the meeting.

Your secretary calls ahead and suggests that the staff be at their desks at 10:30. She later makes the set-up call, and when everyone is on the line rings you on the conference phone. You think how remarkable it is that the new intelligent telephone and PBX can do all of this so quickly and without having to schedule the meeting a day or even a week ahead with the conference operator. The meeting gets underway, and after about 10 minutes it becomes clear that several more people ought to be there. You ask your secretary to call in the extra marketing people and perhaps find the sales rep responsible for this product line. But the rep is somewhere on the other side of town. The secretary pages her, and in about five minutes she is on the line from a telephone booth and participating in the conference.

In about an hour you are off to lunch with a job candidate. There are some tasks you just cannot do remotely, despite your expertise with the telecommunications technologies. Face-to-face, eye-to-eye conversations, ''pressing the flesh'' as politicians often call it, is what is necessary when sizing up a new employee.

About 1:30 P.M. you are back in the office just in time for a meeting with the research project leader who is proposing several new ideas, all of which seem to be terribly risky and expensive. But that's what business is all about. It turns into a long and important meeting that lasts until the late afternoon. The meeting seemed to reach some definite conclusions, but you are puzzled about the printer technology proposed for the product. Indeed, there were some things you did not understand at all. (Has the field gotten away from you?) Your researcher offered to brief you on the new print technology, but you thought you'd like to find out for yourself.

Turning on your desk terminal, you log into one of the information utilities requesting a search for articles, reports, books, and so forth, on "laser printing." It isn't too long before a rather impressive but not overlong list of items is presented in terms of recency of publication. You read a few of the "online" abstracts, get the drift of the concept, then from the same service order copies of two articles.

While you have the terminal up and going, you decide to skip a planned visit to the bank and instead use the "On-line Financial Analysis and Services Network" (OFASN) in order to get ready for tomorrow's budget meeting. You check on some key balances, funds transfers, and request a quarterly profit-loss projection. It's printed out before you clear your desk for the day and you think of how much time you saved by staying out of downtown traffic.

Finally, back in your car and on the freeway home, you set the mobile phone to forward all your calls to your office voice mail system. It takes one more flip of a switch to turn on a Mozart piano concerto and put the world of traffic and the day's more ragged edges behind you.

A typical day for today's executive? Probably not—but the possibilities are all there.

3

MANAGEMENT INNOVATIONS THROUGH TELECOMMUNICATIONS

You cannot run a business, or anything else, on a theory.

Harold S. Geneen, *Managing*

NO SIMPLE THEORY

Like Harold Geneen of ITT fame, we cannot recommend any ''Theory X,'' ''Theory Y,'' or ''The Art of Japanese Management'' as a simple success formula for doing business in the information age. Surely there are ideas from these theories that may work for you, but the assumption that there is one way to manage is as outdated as the success stories of the corporations used as examples for these oversimplified formulas. Most successful managers, as you can learn from biographies or scientific studies of executive excellence, represent individuals who have unique and special insights about their business and who have been able to capitalize on this information for leadership. They have been able to use information to increase the value of themselves and their workers for their business.

Our fundamental premise is that *information* is a critical resource for modern managers.

You must know what information you need and how to get it in order to make a decision.

You must know how to use key information in interaction with your colleagues, consultants, and staff members, in order to get a decision implemented.

You must know how to get information on the consequences of your own and your employees' actions.

With all this emphasis on information, perhaps this is why you spend so much of your day plowing through paperwork, conducting meetings, and just plain talking on the telephone, over the lunch table, and in your office. Indeed, cartoonists have had a field day with the talkative executive—managers with telephones growing out of their ears. Or maybe you've heard the long-time joke that "good executives are born with a telephone in their hands rather than a silver spoon in their mouths."

With so much riding on information-handling skills, the new telecommunications technologies promise significant benefits for the executive who learns how to make the best use of this new array of information tools. Just as the best managers of the industrial revolution were able to develop profitable applications of machines for physical work, the most successful executives of the postindustrial age are those who can harness the new telecommunications and computing technologies for the expansion of human intellectual powers and applications.

Your critical questions of yourself as an executive are direct and simple:

What information will make myself and my staff more valuable to the purpose of our business?

How can I apply the new telecommunications technologies to increase that value?

The answers to these questions require consideration of how information is changing the environment of modern organizations.

HOW TELECOMMUNICATIONS CHANGES WORK

Changes Are Essentially Human

Your first thought (quite naturally) should be one of being a better manager—to be able to make decisions and carry out actions so that your employees are more effective workers. Yet all of this is more than a simple concept of increasing quantity or efficiency. In fact, as we subsequently discuss, simple concepts of efficiency are inadequate for gauging the impact of telecommunications on organization. For example, you may have a great amount of information at your fingertips, yet that information may not be the basis for improved decisions. Indeed, it could result in "information overload," with the consequences of poorer decisions. Nor is just increasing the amount of work per unit time of your typical employee a necessarily desirable aim. The extra work that is accomplished may not contribute in a positive manner to the effectiveness of the organization. The critical goal is to implement changes that benefit the effectiveness of the overall organization, not just isolated operations with it. The key to this is in improving the contributions of managers and workers to that effectiveness. To achieve this improvement requires focusing on people!

The major areas of human impact of information technologies include changes in the organization hierarchy and power structure, in the uses of communications media and information flow, and in employee attitudes about their work. Finally, training is crucial to adapting your organization to the human changes brought about by information work and the increased use of telecommunications.

Three Dimensions of Change

1. *The Organization and Its Power Structure.*   By their very nature, telecommunications technologies often change the organizational structure. Traditionally, many of the communication distinctions in hierarchy and power have been perpetuated by building layouts, office design, seating arrangements within meeting rooms, or even mail routing practices.

The relative geographic or spatial freedom introduced by telecommunications alternatives can invite alternatives to tradition. One frequent contemporary example is the bypassing of organizational levels when managers use desktop computers and local networks to access information directly from their company's databases. This bypasses the traditional distance between the data processing center and the executive offices of an organization. It threatens the power of data processing managers and even comptrollers. Moreover, the executive, even in a lower echelon of management, who knows how to gain direct access to critical information may become more valuable to the organization than a higher echelon individual who is restricted by traditional methods.

To managers on their way up, availability of new information technologies, and primarily the ability to apply them, is increasingly a requirement for corporate success. How the senior executive makes such opportunities available may be one of the most critical factors for corporate change.

2. *Media Uses and Communications Flow.* If the implementation of telecommunications has a desirable effect on an organization, people will begin to communicate differently. This can result in such changes as:

The substitution of one communications medium for another, as in sending certain personal messages by intraoffice electronic mail rather than by telephone or paper memo

Who has access to what information

Increases in the amounts of information available

Easy access to information

Expansions in the span of influence an executive has in interacting with other managers and employees

Intraoffice communications is a typical example of change, namely the substitutability of electronic mail for informal memos or face-to-face conversations. As one examines personal communications in higher levels of the executive hierarchy, it is often the personal skills of the individual that loom important. The ability to quickly exchange information in a face-to-face situation, to exchange nonverbal cues (facial expressions, gestures, and tone of voice), to interact so as to revise thoughts or actions, and to mix exchanges with the business message is often restricted when media are involved. For many years, we have had to adapt to the telephone and its masking of nonverbal cues and communication. We often use language style to compensate for the lack of those more personally oriented cues of "social presence."

These personal factors have been a subject of interest in contemporary studies of electronic mail systems. Several generalizations seem evident. For one, it takes an acquired skill to be able to create electronic messages that have visibly personal and persuasive characteristics. The bias in modern American culture is to use written forms of communication in a more formal manner than speech. Accordingly, when we create messages at a keyboard we are inclined to carry over our old habits. Another generalization is that because of the ease of using distribution lists, many electronic mail systems become overburdened with low priority messages. As a consequence, electronic mail often gains a stereotype of being a vehicle for less important messages.

There is also the keyboard problem. Save for some exceptions, the ability to type has not traditionally been the mark of the executive; in fact, it has been the opposite. Consequently, we should not expect the traditional executive to readily adapt to a technology that requires typing skills for efficient (and comfortable) use.

Meetings are another example of communication changes. They have been the most important setting for interpersonal persuasion, motivation, negotiation, or for any other purposes where especially personalized exchanges are important. What happens, then, when a telecommunications medium replaces a face-to-face context of a meeting? If, for example, the Monday morning sales meeting is replaced by a teleconference, will it have the same motivational impact? If participants have fewer opportunities for personal asides while interacting, if the meeting is fixed to the often more formal agenda of a teleconference, will the same degree of enthusiasm be attained? Experience indicates that unless the participants know one another well and are willing to communicate in an uninhibited fashion, teleconferences are not an effective substitute for face-to-face meetings when motivation or negotiation is involved.

There are also technological consequences on the broad flow of patterns of communications within an organization. As many of you have experienced, if you wanted special data from the company computer, a request given to the data processing manager was required. With new management information systems, many executives have direct access to company databases which, in effect, bypasses the traditional domain of data processing managers and devalues their roles. Direct access to such information can also change the nature of decision-making in the executive suite. Direct use of databases further raises questions as to who should have access to such data, who will check on its accuracy, and, above all, how security will be maintained.

Finally, there is the ''skill'' problem with individuals' changes and uses of communication media. As already mentioned, some individuals are more adept at keyboard use than others. But there are other skill interactions as well. For example, there is the ''Hollywood'' effect that favors some individuals over others in audio-video teleconferencing. Some individuals simply photograph better and hence gain an advantage with the new technology. Indeed, there are some individuals with a certain ''telephone voice and personality'' that can dominate even the impersonal audio-only conference.

Every manager has his or her own management style and the many varieties of media available today allow for that special style to be expressed most effectively. You have the opportunity to select from among the varieties of media those that best suit your particular style for that special interaction or meeting. If we can learn from human experience with media over the years, from print through the telephone, and television to the computer, you will learn what suits you best.

3. *Employee Attitudes.*   Working with new information technologies often has a profound effect on employee attitudes, and these can initially be negative. On a general level are differences in the willingness of individuals to try new media. Personal attitude looms as a critical variable in technological adoption. Frankly, there are more than a few individuals who will never adapt, or the cost of their trials and tribulations to the organization will likely be prohibitive. There are also sizable numbers of individuals who will only ''tolerate'' a change, but never achieve the higher levels of productivity or effectiveness presumably associated with the technological adoption.

It is not unusual to find that an employee's initial experience with a new technology can be a negative one. Despite the promises of acceptance often touted in sales pitches, a common reaction is one of initial resistance or least reluctance, on the part of employees (including many managers). Without developing favorable employee attitudes, you can never be successful with the implementation.

On the clerical level, the introduction of any new way of working is an emotional experience. Most clerical workers will feel that they are being tested by the technology, and particularly in the case of telecommunications, they fear that their performance is easily observable by ''outsiders.'' This holds whether you are introducing a new PBX system, electronic mail, or any kind of technology that involves an essential change in the employee's personal communication behaviors. Although training seminars are of assistance in reducing resistance to information technologies, this is a long-range problem to be ultimately solved by the supervisor or manager.

Moreover, if an organization is already poorly managed, new technology can become a negative rallying point. The problems may not be the technology at all but the circumstances of work that existed before the introduction. In numerous cases, the feared health effects of video display terminal have become a specific rallying point for negative attitudes. As a manager, you should ask your vendor or training organization for help in avoiding this problem before it has a chance to emerge.

Another source of employee dissatisfaction is that supervisors and their managers often do not realize that habits must be changed so as to achieve the most productive (and comfortable) uses of the new technology. There is a need for new "work rhythms." A common example of this is in the adoption of word processing. Because an operator is handling two to three times the textual material handled with traditional typing, a higher level of cognitive attention is required. Unless the employee has regular breaks, stress and fatigue are likely to develop and performance rapidly diminishes. The solution in many cases has been one of replacing the traditional 15 minute morning and afternoon breaks with, say, three 10 minute breaks, preferably one per hour.

Employees also typically resent the fact that some information technologies can maintain a detailed record of their work output. If this is the case in your organization, it will be important to negotiate adoption of such monitoring, and to involve the employees in setting standards.

Employees are often aware of the negative consequences of technology introduction leading to outright obsolescence of jobs, if not "deskilling." Any effective program for information technology implementation must meet this issue head-on. The optimum situation is where employees see opportunities for themselves in the introduction of technologies, such as the upgrading of their job skills, and eventually compensation, as well as the reduction of routine, boring tasks in their work. Perhaps the best way to overcome the initial hurdle of negative employee attitudes is to involve individuals as much as you can in the preparation for the introduction of new telecommunications and computer technologies. In that way, workers can become committed to the success of the innovation and you can then build on that commitment.

As discussed next, training is also a key to developing favorable employee attitudes. But you still have the long-range responsibility of maintaining those attitudes.

Training Is a Key to Change

Training has never been more important than in the introduction of information technologies in the office. Many of the technologies are so different from existing systems that there is often little opportunity for learning to take place "on the floor" from more experienced employees. The acquisition of the new system often requires the additional investment of sending employees to special classes, having on-site training, or simply offering incentives for employees to train themselves. Training is probably the most overlooked component in the implementation of new communications technologies. The more sophisticated the technology, or the more radical the change in the work environment, the more training will be necessary.

Ironically, training is often underemphasized by technology vendors and specialists within the organization who take pride in their position because they have insights about the technology not shared by others. Vendors may wish to encourage you that their equipment is so easily used that very little training will be necessary.

You should also be aware that training with information technologies is not an initial task. To realize the full productivity potential, it is necessary to have a longer-range training program. After employees accomplish initial operations of the new technologies, they should be trained to develop new work habits, and to introduce innovations into the system. In some applications employees can eventually train each other.

Modern training may often have as much to do with organizational change as with the operation of the technology itself. As a consequence, it is important to have the training relate as closely as possible to your unique organizational environment. An implication of this need is that the most effective training often takes place in the employee's work environment rather than in classes far removed from the realities of the job. "Outside" classes may be valuable for general technological know-how (such as how to operate a PBX), but they are often deliberately general in organizational content because they must accommodate individuals from a wide variety of work environments. Such classes are likely to have far more stress on the technology itself than on the important organizational impact and adaptation mentioned above. Remember, too, that these classes may not deal directly with *your* use of the innovation.

Finally, telecommunications technologies themselves offer new opportunities for training. Many types of computer software have built-in tutorial routines, or "help" menus that can answer questions that typically arise with specific operations. It is important also to have help available for more specialized or esoteric questions that may arise. No vendor is really serious about customer support if they do not have a "help" telephone number, especially an "800" one.

If you were around in the days of early computers, you probably vividly remember the frustrations created by poor documentation and almost unreadable training manuals. With the rapid expansion of the telecommunications equipment market, the worlds of documentation and training (or instructional manuals) have not improved much. However, you should not overlook these important assists to more rapid adoption of your new office systems. It might even be worth assigning an employee, or hiring a consultant, to prepare a manual suited to your particular requirements.

INCREASING TELECOMMUNICATIONS PAYOFFS

Limitations of Efficiency Concepts

Efficiency, usually the central concept to productivity, implies the ability to produce "more with less." As applied to telecommunications technology, it could refer to the speed at which telephone calls are routed, decreases in cost of transmission resulting from least cost routing, the more rapid and inexpensive dissemination of electronic mail, or even the lower costs of communication due to installation of your own network. In typical clerical applications, productivity often means increases in work completed, such as a secretary's ability to type and edit more words per hour on a word processor as compared with a traditional typewriter.

All such examples reflect a factory or manufacturing focus on work produced per unit of time, or its calculation in financial terms. The essential limitation of this efficiency concept is that it is not always necessarily related to the needs of an organization. For example, if your new PBX system can handle double the traffic of the old one, this may have a negligible impact on your organization if the traffic is not there. You may have overinvested in a system for which you are not yet ready. You might have done better by growing into your needs. Furthermore, you may have placed a burden on the operator that could result in a new set of tensions leading to other inefficiencies around the office.

Obviously, efficiency is an important component in increasing telecommunications payoff, but without relating it to the overall operation of the organization, there is no assured payoff. A more encompassing concept is required, one that analysts (e.g., Paul Strassmann) call "effectiveness."

Effectiveness as a "Value Added" Concept

Whereas efficiency applies to particular acts or operations within an organization, *effectiveness* is a more encompassing concept that refers to the overall operation of the organization. Recall the concept of "management as an information-intensive activity," as first illustrated in Chapter 1 (Figure 1.1) and described in more detail in Chapter 2 (Table 2.3). With this concept in mind, consider how, in abstract terms, the essential function of the business organization is one of *value added*. That is, given the difference between input cost (e.g., raw materials, labor, and services), and output price (the product or service), what added value has been contributed by the organization's activities?

All investments, including capital as well as operating costs, presumably "purchase" the value added by the organization. Consequently, all facets of costs, such as the contributions of employees, managers, as well as technologies, to value added offers a criterion for gauging effectiveness. *Put into practical terms, if an investment in telecommunications technology is made for an organization, what is its contribution to organizational value added?* For example, even if the efficiency of message distribution in an organization is doubled because of the addition of a local area network, what is the contribution of that efficiency increase as value added to the operation of the organization?

In overall terms, all investments in the operation of the organization, including the addition of telecommunications and the management of it, should be ultimately gauged in terms of their value added, a specific criterion of effectiveness. Again, effectiveness is an organizational concept, whereas efficiency reflects a focus on specific activities within that organization.

In the present concept of effectiveness, it is important to bear in mind that the overall concept of value added is set relative to prices of products or services that the market will support. This is a particularly useful concept because certain investments in technologies, even with very similar records of operating efficiency, may be much more effective under some market conditions than others. Essentially, if the market prices are high, and the value added over the organizational operation is consequently high, the effectiveness of the telecommunications investment will be increasingly attractive. Or put into negative terms, as market prices decline for a product or services, telecommunications investments may practically reach a point where no payoff will be possible. Managers who do not know their markets cannot make sound investments in telecommunications.

Every manager must decide for himself or herself just what factors are critical to the success of the operation, what factors if improved will generate the effectiveness being sought. Another way of looking at this is to ask just where in the business can the greatest value be realized. You may decide, for example, that more frequent contact with your sales staff is critical to the improvement of income and that an electronic mail system coupled with more frequent teleconferences will accomplish this goal. Ultimately, the worth of this investment in technology and its management must be gauged by value added relative to changes in your sales staff's activities. There is a distinctly human component to effectiveness.

The Goal: Increasing Human Potential for Value Added

Humans, more so than telecommunications technologies themselves, are the necessary focus for increasing telecommunications payoffs. To what degree does the technology amplify the contribution of the worker? To what degree does the technology enhance the contribution of the manager? The cost of human participation in the form of wages and benefits typically far exceeds the investment in the technology itself. Technology cannot be integrated into the organization without the assistance of human skills and talents. In essence, telecommunications payoff comes in terms of increasing the value added by workers and managers.

The foregoing is an important premise for executives because ultimately differences in gaining telecommunications payoffs are going to be far more affected by the capabilities of people working for you than by the basic capabilities of the technology. This means that you must be more of a specialist in guiding human behavior than a technologist. The new challenge is one of increasing the added value of managers and workers in your organization. *Information technologies are tools and not ends in this process.*

In the most practical of terms, the two key questions you need to answer are:

1. Relative to valued added effectiveness, is it likely that the purchase of telecommunications equipment or services will result in the payoffs you want?
2. Given a payoff goal, what management activities will be required to achieve it?

Once again, these questions simply emphasize that the acquisition of technology is not a guarantee of success. *Telecommunications payoff requires management.*

GUIDELINES FOR IMPLEMENTATION OF TELECOMMUNICATIONS

1. *Analyze Your Organization.*   Two of the most frequent problems found in the implementation of telecommunications are: (1) the critical information-handling operations have gone unanalyzed, having been typically relegated to overhead, and (2) when technology is implemented, it simply "fixes" a potentially inefficient system that is already in place. Ask first what are your primary needs for information within your organization, and in particular, what is their relation with value added effectiveness as previously described. Given a decision as to your information priorities, only then ask how technology can serve these needs.

2. *Set Strategic Goals.*   Knowing what you generally expect to accomplish from your telecommunications acquisitions, set specific goals for performance. Express these goals so that they can eventually be interpreted relative to value added effectiveness of workers and managers. This means that you must have accurate estimates of costs and payoffs. Do not overlook all aspects of personnel costs, including training.

3. *Write Technology Specifications in Terms of Functions.*   It will be

distinctly to your advantage in dealing with vendors if you have an explicit description of your telecommunications requirements. Write specifications in terms of functions to be accomplished and level of expected performance rather than in terms of specific brands or models of equipment (except for examples). Specifications also include your ranges of anticipated cost. Be sure that software, subsequent modification, and especially employee training are included in your specifications.

4. *Take Advantage of a Buyer's Market.* Currently and probably until the end of the century, it will be a buyer's market in telecommunications technology, particularly in terms of growth of global competition. Because it is a buyer's market, you can gain the insights of different experienced vendors in evaluating your specifications. It is possible that you may wish to modify your specifications as you gain experience with bids. Because the market is so competitive, you will have advantages in negotiating the addition of training and evaluation or subsequent equipment replacement as a part of your contract.

Because telecommunications technology itself is undergoing such rapid change with new equipment offering better services, often at lower costs, the buyer's market will enable you to move especially wisely to acquire what you need. You will be able to consider a host of options such as leasing, by which you will be able to always keep up with the latest systems that might better meet your needs.

5. *Evaluate Results and Set New Goals.* If you have effectively planned for new telecommunications, you will in all likelihood be expecting changes in how you operate your organization. You will want to evaluate such changes against anticipated goals and thereby determine the degree to which you are achieving your desired effectiveness. No predictions of effectiveness are entirely accurate, so in order to maximize your benefits from your new telecommunications, you should undertake evaluation with the anticipation that you may be able to achieve still greater benefits.

The greatest failings in telecommunications implementation are not in the technologies but typically in the failure of managers and workers to apply the technologies for their optimum benefits. As a consequence, the successful executive will consider evaluation and goal revision as an ongoing process. If evaluation is done properly, it should give you increased insights into the value added component of your specific technology investments.

PART TWO

NEW TELECOMMUNICATIONS FOR MANAGING BETTER

4
THE INTELLIGENT TELEPHONE

YOUR INDISPENSABLE BUSINESS MACHINE

The telephone is your most important information instrument. No longer does it simply connect you to another party for a conversation; it has become intelligent. That is, today's telephone can coordinate, schedule, and manage your communications. Perhaps not as efficiently as your personal secretary, but how many of today's managers can have an efficient and intelligent personal secretary that never sleeps?

Consider the following situation:

A small market research and public relations firm with relatively few clients is successful because they spend a great deal of time with each client. The staff is always on the telephone with these clients, calling them many times during the day. When public relations campaigns are underway these calls are even more frequent. Many outside and part-time consultants are employed to keep overhead down, but this results in a heavy telephone bill. The firm is attractive because their chief executive gives the clients her personal attention; she is always there when important decisions are made. For this company, the telephone is their most valuable communication and information instrument. There are heavy demands on their receptionist: to place calls,

to locate wandering staff and consultants, to arrange teleconferences,
and so forth. Telephone tag is no longer a game, it is a problem.

DOING AWAY WITH TELEPHONE TAG

There are four solutions to the telephone tag problem:

1. Hire a very intelligent and hardworking receptionist equipped with a desktop electronic switchboard.
2. Subscribe to Centrex services.
3. Purchase or lease a PBX.
4. Purchase or lease intelligent telephones.

The first solution is the tried but not too true solution. Your voice to the outside world soon becomes strained as your receptionist becomes overloaded and customers hear that. And, the cost is high.

The second solution shifts the burden of managing your telephone communications to the local telephone carrier. Centrex has become a generic term for a telephone central office switch into which you can connect as part of your local telephone services. Centrex can provide you with as many as 40 different services, such as call forwarding and the like, as well as assist you in monitoring your costs and thereby controlling your costs. With Centrex services you have no capital investment, no hardware, and no maintenance headaches. All of the switching equipment is in the telephone central office. You lease just what you need and as you expand your operations, you can lease additional lines and services. When new developments come online you can lease them, too. What you do not get is control over just how you want to use these services and the ability to program special adaptations that might be unique to your operations. Since these services are tariffed by the state utility commissions you also do not have control over rates. Given the present flexible state of the telephone industry your rates may go up when you least expect them or want them to.

The third solution brings the Centrex, or some smaller version into your office. While you gain control over costs and over the services you want and may design for yourself, you do acquire the burden of a capital investment, of maintenance, of finding a place for the hardware, and of keeping on top of new developments. Internal PBX's come in a variety of sizes, but are not cost-effective unless you have approximately 250 or more telephones in your facility. If you are planning on introducing data into your office or plant communications networks you will want to seriously consider the modern voice/data PBX which we shall discuss in the next chapter.

THE INTELLIGENT TELEPHONE SOLUTION

The fourth solution takes advantage of the new line of electronic telephones that have a good deal of intelligence built into the instruments themselves. This intelligence enables you to program your telephone for many, but certainly not all of the functions you may expect either from Centrex or your own PBX. You program these telephones by resetting switches on the program cards in the instrument and by adding additional program cards on which the program has been installed. This way of packing software is often called firmware. While you can have a great deal of flexibility in designing the services you need, you may have to assume the responsibility of maintaining the telephones. And your expansion capabilities may be limited; should you want to integrate data into your voice communications and expand the number of lines to, say, 100, you will likely have to consider other alternatives. But for a firm with 20 to 60 lines for primarily voice communications, the intelligent telephone solution may be ideal.

This is the solution adopted by our market research firm. Prior to issuing a request for proposal they did some research and came up with the analysis of their needs shown in Table 4.1.

TRAINING IS IMPORTANT

You are likely to find the training manuals provided by your telephone supplier so poorly written as to be useless. It is best to obtain a temporary training consultant to prepare manuals that suit your needs and the ''cheat sheets'' or small instruction cards that can be attached to every telephone. Additionally, several training sessions should be scheduled.

Table 4.1 *Analysis of Telephone Communications Requirements*

System Equipment	"At Cut"[a]	"Wired"[b]	Function	Operational Benefits
Voice ports	40	50	Access to telephone network for all staff	Provides for a telephone at every desk
Voice instruments single line	35	35	Access for junior staff	Provides capability for junior staff to perform most of their one-on-one functions
Multiple lines	15	25	Access for senior staff	Provides capability for senior staff to access multiple offices simultaneously
"Hands free" instruments	5	8	Eliminates need for lifting handset until party speaks	Place call without lifting handset, frees hands to continue writing until call begins
Conference telephones	1	2	For audio teleconferencing. Future video conferencing	Replaces in-office meetings when difficult to assemble all parties, eliminates scheduling frustrations
Data ports	20	25	For accessing data bases; voice/data integration not required now	Provides capability for accessing online data bases, provides for future electronic messaging and document transfers
Broadband ports	1	2	For future video teleconferencing and high speed data	Video displays of artwork and other documents and provides for high speed data communications when needed

42

System Software

Feature	Function	Benefit
Call forwarding 1. To the switchboard after three rings 2. To another extension after three rings 3. Programmable to either 1 or 2 4. To another location; home, etc.	Programs telephone to forward your incoming calls to a selected phone in office or calls home or to receptionist	Reduces telephone tag; allows for mobility and connectivity, keeps managers in touch at all times and at all places.
Multiple intercom dialing	Programs telephone to act as intercom, allows you to reach multiple parties	Attracts attention of party interrupting online conversation, important in emergencies
Night ringing at stations when office switchboard is closed	Transfers incoming calls to specified executive or project leader when office is closed or receptionist away from desk	Helps prevent loss of potential client or important emergency call
Call conference (3 to 6 parties)	Sets up an audio teleconference with 3 or 6 people, operator not needed	Enables staff to conference as needed and when necessary with in-house and home workers, call in experts as needed
Call transfer 1. To another station 2. To switchboard	Transfers incoming call to another party or to receptionist to page or take message	Ensures that right person gets call or allows for more appropriate party to respond to inquiry, receptionist can take over task of finding party or getting message to party
Call waiting-tone (programmable at station)	Informs you when a second call is waiting while you are on line	Tells second party that you are putting party on hold or more important, terminate first call, make arrangement to call back

Table 4.1 (Continued)

System Equipment	"At Cut"[a]	"Wired"[b]	Function	Operational Benefits
Listen on hold			When on hold, you can work "hands free" until called party is on line	Saves valuable waiting time, increases productivity
Speed calling			Programs frequently called numbers so they are automatically dialed	Stores up to 70 numbers for fast dialing, especially useful for frequently called clients, no need to lift handset to dial
Ring again			When busy signal is encountered, will notify you when line is available and dial again	Saves time redialing, allows you to continue work while waiting for open line, improves productivity
Station restrictions on long distance dialing			Programs phones for specific distance calling	Saves money by reserving long distance for those whose jobs require long distance calls

Maintenance terms:
Maintenance to be provided by supplier contract

Training and instruction terms:
Provisions for staff and management training including appropriate training materials and instructions

Special requirements:
Air conditioning, grounding, battery venting, colocations with electrical systems, weight, size, and space requirements to be kept at minimum

[a] "At cut"—all aspects are operational at installation.
[b] "Wired"—all internal central processing unit wiring, if any, and program cards available.
The total system should be capable of expansion simply with the addition of wiring, program cards, and appropriate software modifications.

WHAT'S NEXT FOR YOUR INTELLIGENT TELEPHONE SYSTEM?

In this new highly competitive telecommunications environment, the carriers are going to offer incentives for customers to use their services and to do so they are going to provide opportunities for more and more equipment to use their transmission lines and switches. Consequently you will see an almost daily deluge of newly integrated voice data terminals (IVDT) on the marketplace. Some will require you to bring more of the carriers' intelligence into your office by way of the PBX. This will be especially true if you want to integrate your voice and data communications. Others will provide an increasing amount of intelligence in the telephone itself so that you will not need to have your own PBX but can use the telephone company's services. This is a trade-off you will have to make, the trade-off between rather large capital investments for more intelligence in your office versus considerably less that enables you to share the intelligence tasks with the carriers' intelligent telephone system.

Keeping track of the varieties of equipment coming on the market is almost a full-time job. An excellent source that will keep you abreast of the changes taking place as well as many interesting case stories of how users are solving their problems can be found in *Communications News*, a monthly magazine published by

> Harcourt Brace Jovanovich
> 124 South First Street
> Geneva, Illinois 60134

and in *Telecommunications*, also a monthly magazine, published by

> Horizon House-Microwave, Inc.
> 610 Washington Street
> Dedham, Massachusetts 02026

5

THE VOICE/DATA PBX

INTEGRATION OF VOICE AND DATA FOR EFFECTIVE MANAGEMENT

Following the introduction of the new voice/data PBX in his office, Karl, the vice president of sales, discovered a new way of doing business. In the past, department heads would submit their proposed bids for major projects to him for approval in writing. He would often take them home and make comments in the margin and return them for appropriate modification. More recently these proposals were delivered to him via the electronic mail network and he would send his comments back via the electronic mail network. Now he uses his integrated voice/data terminal to call the sender either directly or via voice mail and responds to the electronic message with a voice message. Karl figures that this has cut his review time in half and, furthermore, feels more secure that his suggestions are received, understood, and followed.

The dominant form of communications in the office is and will continue to be by voice, over the telephone, in face-to-face meetings, and in teleconferences. Managers rate the telephone and face-to-face communications as their most preferred and most used forms of communications. Yet, managers have an increasing need to find more efficient ways to run their organizations, and are putting new demands on telecommunications technology mainly because they want the power that comes from communicating with freedom and flexibility.

Information in the modern office comes in many forms: voice communications, written memos, illustrated reports, elaborate audiovisual presentations, and data. Information may be exchanged symmetrically, that is in real time, as are voice communications on the telephone, or asymmetrically, as they are when memoranda are sent through the mails. Telecommunications must be able to handle all forms of communication modes and timing. Networks must be designed to be able to exchange information among a variety of devices using voice, data, and even video.

Managing effectively and productively with the new telecommunications requires that you have the ability to choose the right technology for the job and be able to quickly access that technology conveniently. That's why the new IVDTs are appearing in the marketplace. Couple these intelligent terminals with the software controlled or intelligent network, and you can have the ability to fully manage your own telecommunications. It is this ability that can give you the competitive edge over the competition made possible by the new telecommunications. But first you must determine if you need the higher power and the higher cost of a voice/data PBX.

HOW THE VOICE/DATA PBX FITS INTO YOUR PLANS

The PBX is the equipment that helps you manage your private voice communications, just as the old switchboard and operator did. If you do not have a sufficient number of telephones in your office to warrant a PBX you could use the intelligent telephone (as illustrated in the previous chapter), transferring some of the switchboard functions to your electronic telephone. Another way of managing your voice communications in your office, especially when you have relatively few telephones (less than 50) is to purchase service rather than hardware by accessing PBX intelligence at the telephone central office, a Centrex system. These PBX's, either in your office or at the telephone office, even if digitally switched as most of them are today, are designed to meet your voice communications requirements.

However, data communications in the office are increasing and you need to be able to deal with the asymmetrical communications of data as well as the symmetrical voice communications. The leap to systems that can handle both voice and data communications is a long and often expensive one, requiring careful appraisal of your needs. The modern voice/data PBX is a complex system capable of a great deal of flexibility.

The voice/data PBX integrates telephones, computers, voice messaging systems, computer messaging systems, word processors, printers, connects you to the public switched telephone network, to a public data network such as Telenet or Tymenet, to specialized common carriers such as MCI, Sprint, and AT&T for long distance services, and to a variety of additional equipment that your multimedia office requires. Figure 5.1 illustrates the flexibility of the modern voice/data PBX.

Today's voice/data PBXs are really large computers with an enormous variety of features paralleling those that can be offered by the telephone company Centrex systems. These features are usually divided up into system features, including those the intelligent tele-

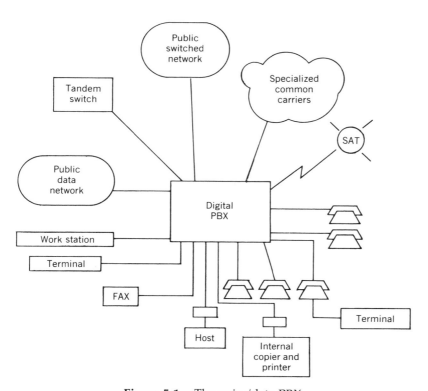

Figure 5.1. The voice/data PBX

phone offers (see Chapter 4) and much more. Here are some of the more important features you will find on a voice/data PBX, features that are not available via your intelligent telephone, and in some cases, not available from Centrex services:

Least Cost Routing. Finding the least cost path for your long distance telephone call. (Not available from Centrex.)

Voice Store and Forward. Sending voice messages that are stored and wait to be picked up by the recipient, another solution to the telephone tag problem. (Not available from Centrex.)

Data Terminal Interfaces. Data communications between terminals at speeds up to 64 kilobits/second.

Access to Digital Trunks. Data communications for interplant and interoffice at speeds up to 2.048 megabits/second.

RS-232-C Compatibility. For operation with terminal devices equipped with an RS-232-C interface, for example, personal computers.

Special Purpose Software. Depending on your business you can have software built in, for example, hotel/motel lodging packages.

Account Call Capability. Keeps a record of all calls and prepares reports for review of telecommunications expenses.

Network Administration. Allows you to control your entire network.

Programmable Stations. You can program the services for each station in your firm, and when a person changes offices, the program can be shifted to the new telephone.

Radio Paging. Built-in capability for direct paging when requested.

Stored Program Control. For high speed switching, especially for data communications.

Expandability. Ability to grow with your needs.

Every function described for the intelligent telephone is vastly expanded by the voice/data PBX. Consequently, a voice/data PBX is a major piece of equipment, often requiring air conditioning in your location and while its reliability is high, you will want to have your own maintenance staff on board. After all you will be putting all of your telecommunications capability in this equipment. The decision to purchase this system requires careful thought and a considerable amount of analysis.

Ten Questions to Answer Before You Purchase a Voice/Data PBX

Before you jump into this world of voice/data integration, here are 10 questions you and your staff should think about.

1. Are communications, particularly data communications, a major part of the products and services that generate revenue for your company? Are you a financial services firm, a real estate operation, engineering consultant, a travel agent, in short, an information intensive business?

2. What is the current percentage mix of voice versus data traffic locally? In the metropolitan area? In long distance communications?

3. What relative growth rates do you expect for voice and data traffic over the next 2 years, 5 years, 10 years?

4. How is the traffic distributed as to distance? What is the voice traffic likely to be locally? In the metropolitan area? Over long distance? What is the data traffic likely to be over these areas?

5. Of the current and forecast traffic, what percentage is not readily compatible with today's voice switching methods? Many of today's standard or nondata PBXs and Centrex services are digitally switched and, consequently, can handle data speeds up to about 9600 bits per second. Also new Centrex services are always increasing their abilities to route high speed traffic.

6. Given your answer to question 5, do you consider voice/data integration desirable for both switching and transmission facilities or for one or the other separately? You can save a great deal of money if you determine that digital switching is adequate for your needs.

7. Are communications split between voice and data in your company particularly at the local level? Are voice and data communications managed by different entities in your corporation? Are corporate communications perceived to be complex, costly, and difficult to manage? Your decision to integrate voice and data communications may lead to significant

management difficulties; certainly a considerable amount of education may be required.

8. Is your objective to reduce short-term costs or to plan for efficiency and cost control over the long run?

9. Is your objective to seek new markets and develop new products for which telecommunications and, in particular, integrated voice and data communications are important?

10. Are you prepared for a major reorganization of your management structure, likely to result from integrating voice and data communications?

WHAT THE VOICE/DATA PBX CAN DO FOR YOU

One of the biggest challenges managers face is to ensure that office systems can exchange information among fully compatible devices. You will be purchasing equipment from different vendors. One solution is the local area network (LAN), which we shall discuss in Chapter 8. You will find that LAN requires significant engineering and operating talents even if it gives you a great degree of flexibility. The voice/data PBX however can be purchased essentially "off the shelf" with a great variety of special services. Furthermore, with the assistance of the system provider, you can add new functions as you need them. You will be able to communicate voice as well as data and you will save money on modems.

The intelligent telephone interconnects people but you need more than people in order to manage effectively. You need to integrate people with information in order to stay ahead of the competition. The voice/data PBX schedules, manages, and coordinates your information.

6

LONG DISTANCE NETWORKS

THE LONG DISTANCE NETWORK MAZE

Yes, it is confusing. Yes, sometimes what looks like a bargain does not turn out to be one. Yes, it may not be to your advantage to disregard the new long distance service providers of other common carriers (OCCs), to distinguish them from AT&T. On the other hand, it may be the right decision. Or should you acquire a wide area telecommunications service (WATS)? How do you choose among these alternatives? And just what are the alternatives you should seriously examine?

One thing is clear: it is not a simple choice. It is even difficult to determine just who are the providers of long distance telephone services. A service you heard about last month turns out to be an offering only if the provider can get the financing. And some of the providers seem to offer services limited to a region rather than across the nation. And just which of the providers of long distance services offer services internationally?

In the restructuring of the nation's telephone system, calls that go between designated exchange areas, even if they are within the same state or county, are delivered by long distance service providers. Because the term "long distance" may be thought to refer only to calls across state lines or international boundaries, it is better to use the term "interexchange" carriers, and in that we include

Table 6.1. Major Interexchange Service Providers

Allnet
Argo Communications
AT&T Communications
GTE Sprint
ITT/United States Transmission Systems
MCI
Skyline/Satellite Business Systems
UTCI/U.S. Telephone
Telesaver ITT Long Distance
RCI Corporation
Western Union Long Distance Service

all of the services, between exchanges, across state boundaries, and across international boundaries.

It is a maze. Even if it does often appear that the market has calmed down, you should check with your business directory and your colleagues to find out if new providers have been added to the list or if those in Table 6.1 are still in business. In any case, start with this listing of major interexchange carriers.

HOW TO FIND YOUR WAY THROUGH THE LONG DISTANCE TELEPHONE MAZE

There is fierce competition among these services. They compete in price, coverage or connectivity, service quality, customer responsiveness, and how quickly they can offer equal access. But not all of these are of equal importance to your choice of carrier. Clearly, you need to do some serious homework before you buy your long distance services. The following are the key issues you must consider.

Know What Your Interexchange Services Requirements Are

Your first task is to carefully examine your interexchange calling needs. List those cities to which you are likely to be placing most of your calls. Keep in mind that in the new industry structure, calls within your state may require an interexchange carrier. Since you can sign up and be online in a matter of days, or at most within a month of requesting the service, you do not have to speculate far into the future. You can also disconnect most of these services on 30 days' notice.

Ranking the cities you call will also be important; not all of the new interexchange carriers reach every city in the country. And if there are foreign cities on your list, remember that it may be some time before several of these new carriers offer international service.

Take a Realistic Look at the Discounts

In order to encourage competition to AT&T Communications, Inc. (the old AT&T Long Lines) the Federal Communications Commission (FCC) reduced the charges the other common carriers (OCCs) pay for access to the local exchanges. This allows the OCCs to offer a variety of pricing structures and, further, for these prices to move freely in the marketplace. AT&T Communications, Inc. still must go through the FCC for approval of its tariffs and this often takes time. In this way, the FCC hopes to create a "level playing field" for all of the carriers. But until that happens, you will see a great deal of price competition among the OCCs and also periodic price reductions by AT&T Communications as the FCC approves them. Some providers have a minimum monthly charge that might be anywhere from $5 to $25. But under certain conditions and at certain times they might waive this minimum. All offer discounts but they vary with the time of the call. So if you are expecting a 50 percent reduction in your long distance telephone charges you may have to call between 7:00 P.M. and 8:00 A.M. to get this discount. But even this varies with the number of calls you make. Above a certain number of calls you receive a discount across all time periods.

Your toll calls will certainly exceed the monthly minimum so you will be paying only for the calls you make and will qualify for the many discounts offered. Other factors, such as those that we discuss below, will probably be more important to your choice of interexchange carrier. Compare your monthly OCC costs with the cost of WATS, keeping in mind that you can "rent" time on a reseller's WATS line or you can even resell excess time on your own WATS line.

Interexchange rates on the OCCs as well as AT&T are likely to fluctuate rapidly and often. You must keep on top of them in order to control costs. Because the advertising for interexchange services stresses the discounts and WATS calls are not individually charged for, people tend to think that long distance calling is either free or inexpensive. You will have to educate your staff that this is not so and monitor their use.

Do You Call Out-of-the Way Places?

Not all of the services can reach into every town or village in the country, although they are all striving to do so. Only AT&T Communications, the granddaddy of long distance services, can give you that high level of connectivity.

Reaching the cities that rank highest on your list in the United States is likely to be your most important criterion for choice. It is not at all certain that all the OCCs will parallel the reach of AT&T. But this may not be of great concern to you since for those out-of-the-way places your business may periodically need to reach, you will still be able to use AT&T. Alternative interexchange services are most valuable for those frequently called locations where your activities are concentrated.

Does Your Business Require Heavy International Calling?

There are also differences among the OCCs and between them and AT&T in international calling. AT&T is, by far, the primary international telephone carrier, but you can expect that within the next several years most if not all of the OCCs will enter the international exchange market in competition with AT&T. But this requires them to make arrangements with a foreign telephone company, which is difficult because many foreign carriers are government owned monopolies and sometimes not responsive to rapid changes in the marketplace.

The major OCCs are negotiating with the government owned telephone organizations in Western Europe and Japan for access to their networks. Because the terms of access are just now being established it is not clear if the rates the international OCCs will offer will be substantially different from those offered by AT&T.

Keep in Mind that Quality of Service Is Still Improving

It has taken considerable time for the OCC networks to reach the general quality of the over 100 year old AT&T Long Lines. The new interexchange networks use microwave links along various rights-of-way, such as railroads, which often are not as direct as the carriers established by AT&T. Further, interconnection at the AT&T central offices or switching centers has always been difficult. Indeed, the entire question of access to the local exchanges by the new interexchange carriers and the technical quality of the interconnect has been the subject of a long legal dispute. Early users of the new interexchange carriers often complained about echoes, cross-talk, and disconnects. Much of this has been essentially solved and you can expect increasingly high-quality service in the future.

You will need touchtone dialing in order to use the OCC services until equal access becomes a reality. (Equal access will be discussed later in this chapter.) However, there are adaptors that you can attach to your rotary telephones in order to use the OCC long distance services.

As new subscribers come on line in response to the OCCs' advertising campaigns, users complain of long waits for the computer carrier tone necessary for them to input their user code and place their call. This may be especially important if you have automatic dialing equipment. Programmed delays sometimes do not wait for the computer tone and will input your code before the tone. You will have to place the call again. This can become frustrating, especially during the busy calling hours and when the OCCs have not yet added additional computer ports to receive the new subscribers. Service quality is important to you if you are using intelligent telephones or other automatic dialing equipment, such as those you might have on your PBX. On the other hand, the more sophisticated your inhouse telephone system, or your LAN, the more likely it can be programmed to deal with a variety of interexchange system characteristics. Indeed, one of the more important features of the modern PBX is its ability to select from among several interexchange services to give the least cost routing for the call.

Always Plan a Back-Up Service

AT&T will probably be your back-up service for some time to come. After all, AT&T Communications reaches into every city in the nation, regardless of size. It was AT&T that pioneered universal service. Additionally, during those periods when the OCC computer does not respond, your automatic dialing system, or you, will very likely shift to AT&T in order to get the call through. But if the major burden of your interexchange calls is placed on any of the discount services, you are saving money.

Equal Access Will Greatly Simplify Your Interexchange Calling

When you call long distance using AT&T Communications, you dial 1, the area code you are calling, and the number you are calling. But when you use, say, the GTE Sprint services, you may have to dial a Sprint local access number, your access code, the area code you are calling, and the number you are calling. Let's add up the numbers you are dialing:

For AT&T	1-(xxx)xxx-xxxx	11 numbers
For Sprint	xxx-xxxx,xxxxxx-1-(xxx)xxx-xxxx	24 numbers

Equal access requires that you select a primary interexchange carrier. If you select, for example, MCI as your primary carrier, you will dial as you now dial AT&T, dial 1 and the area code and number you are calling. If, for a particular call, you wish to use AT&T, you dial 1-0-ATT or 1-0-288.

COMPETITION IN TELECOMMUNICATIONS WORKS FOR YOU

While there may be a great deal of confusion about who benefits from the restructuring of the nation's telecommunications structure, it is clear that long distance calling can be a bargain for you. Here is a checklist of how you can assure yourself that you are getting the best bargain in long distance calling.

Survey Your Long Distance Calling Requirements

Take a careful inventory of your likely long distance calling requirements. List the cities you call most frequently, beginning with those most frequently called.

Shop Before You Buy

There are probably many colleagues who have great stories about their long distance telephone experiences with AT&T and the

OCCs. Discuss their experiences, keeping a close ear to how they rate service quality. Submit your list of most called cities to several of the OCCs and to AT&T and have them give you a cost estimate based on your listing. Do not overlook WATS, your own or shared. Compare and then buy.

Keep Track of Your Long Distance Calling Costs

Bargains soon disappear if your staff equates bargain rates with free calls. Control your costs by controlling your staff. Remember, you can save even more money if you make your calls at the reduced rate times.

Review Your Purchasing Decision Periodically

Remember, you are not tied into a long-term contract with any of these service providers. And remember, new OCC offerings are made frequently and prices and discounts are subject to changes. Remember, too, that your calling patterns will also be changing. You are not tied into a long-term contract with your long distance provider or providers and you can discontinue on 30 days' notice. So keep track of your costs and reevaluate your purchase often, at least every 6 months, or even more frequently if you note a great deal of movement on the marketplace.

7
PERSONAL COMPUTER COMMUNICATIONS

A NEW WORLD AT YOUR FINGERTIPS

In the beginning the personal computer was treated as a hobbyist kit, then used for games and education, and soon for word processing, databases, and spreadsheets. In the next few years, we may see personal computers used more for communication than they are now used for calculation or even word processing. It is not difficult to equip a personal computer for communications. Without complicated training you can use it for such diverse applications as checking sales figures in the company mainframe, sending or receiving "electronic" mail, consulting airline schedules, transferring funds, checking stock prices, or doing research on patents with information directly from the Patent Office files.

The advantage of using a personal computer rather than a traditional "dumb" terminal for communications is that you can combine the "stand alone" power of word processing, spreadsheet calculations, or database analyses with the ability to send and receive information. The memos that you create with your word processing program can easily be dispatched over the telephone network as electronic mail. The sales data you "download" from your company's minicomputer can be analyzed at your personal convenience with a spreadsheet program. Or if in the midst of your pump re-design, chances are that there is an online database you can consult via your personal computer in a matter of minutes.

61

Personal computer communications offers expanding opportunities for the innovative manager—not only in your activities but in implementation for your staff. In many respects the growth of these opportunities has outstripped the ability of managers to keep up with them. Also there are misapprehensions about the complexities or expenses involved. The facts are that:

Personal computer communications is hardly more complicated than making an ordinary telephone call. You need know nothing about programming to use it.

You do not need highly complex or expensive equipment. Beyond the price of the computer, you can have most personal computers communicating for professional applications for less than a $1000 investment in equipment and programs.

Communications costs are inexpensive. You can "talk" with another computer user often for less than the price of a voice phone call if you use special network options. Costs of "information utilities" are often a bargain compared with the time and costs of locating print material. And there is no "telephone tag" when you exchange messages by electronic mail.

It is easy to subscribe to multipurpose information utilities (see Chapter 12) that offer a wide range of services and databases. These information sources may be anywhere in the country or even the world, but you dial into them as you would dial a local telephone number. When compared with the time your assistant might spend hunting down what you want in the local library or even in old newspapers, the cost will be very attractive.

WHAT YOU NEED FOR PERSONAL COMMUNICATIONS

1. *The Computer.* Virtually any personal computer can be equipped for communication, especially models designed for business use. Some computers, especially the new generation of "lap portables," come with communications capabilities built in. However, you will have the greatest variety of business oriented programs available for you if you invest in a machine that operates with an "MS-DOS" system (the one made standard by the widespread use of the IBM-PC).

Your easiest method of getting equipped for communications is to have your dealer do the job. Whether you take that alternative or not, the necessary additions are described next.

2. *Communications Port.* Although brands of personal computers differ on this feature, you will need circuitry for an input-output "port" for communications. Typically this is called an "RS-232" or "serial" port. For an internally installed modem, this port will be out of sight and the only external connection will be your telephone jack. But if you are to use an external modem, the serial port appears as a 25-pin plug or socket usually installed on the back of your computer. (Serial ports may also be installed for printer connections.)

3. *Modem.* A "modem" (short for "modulator-demodulator") converts your computer's electronic signals into acoustic patterns that can travel over telephone lines. Your best option is a "direct connect" unit that plugs into the telephone network rather than using acoustic cups to fit your telephone handset. If the unit can be installed inside your computer case, all the better. The best modems give you a choice of transmission speeds, generally at either 300 or 1200 bits per second (or "baud"). If you want to use higher speeds, say, 4800 baud or better, you may have to obtain a specially "prepared" telephone line at a higher cost than the regular telephone line or you will end up with a great deal of interference.

Finally, you'll want a modem that is programmable so you can use computer software for automatic dialing, log on sequences, or even auto answering. Often modems and communications programs configured for them can be purchased as a single package. Although there are many excellent modems on the market, you may wish to purchase one that is "Hayes compatible" because software for automatic use as well as sophisticated multifunctional programs (e.g., 1-2-3 or framework) is easily configured for its use.

4. *Communications Software.* Professional level communication uses require programs that allow you to transfer files in and out of your computer, as well as automate functions, such as dialing and others previously mentioned above. Multipurpose or "integrated" programs come with communications capabilities as one of their features. These have the added advantage of being accessible without the need to remove an existing program and load a special communications one. Or a "windowing" system like IBM's "Topview"

allows easy access to a communications program if one has been installed for operation.

You may also wish to consider "bulletin board" software that allows your computer to be used via remote telephone connection. This is discussed in a subsequent section of this chapter.

PUT PERSONAL COMPUTER COMMUNICATIONS TO USE FOR YOU

Some Examples of Innovative Uses

Part Three of this book introduces "Tele-" services, the new applications made available to you via the telephone and the computer. Although the telephone was originally designed for voice communications, engineers have adapted it well for the transmission of computer text, numbers, and information of most any type. This extends the uses of computing and information exchange to the limits of the telephone network. The examples that follow are just a small sample of how a manager can become more efficient by adding computer communications to his or her menu of communication modes.

Moreover, the cost of communicating with computers, providing you use the relatively low speeds of 300 or 1200 baud, is usually no more than the cost of a voice call, and sometimes less. Many of the information utilities and electronic mail services offer a local number from which you can dial anywhere in the country for the cost of a local call. You pay for the information and the mail services and not for the computer telephone call.

One of the most fascinating aspects of computer communications is that there is virtually something in it for everybody. Here are some enthusiastic reports from professional users of different communication services.

Tom is on the road one week each month managing a team of building inspectors. He originally bought one of the new "lap" portable computers so he could draft his reports on the plane. For a few months, he would wait until he got back to the office to print out a draft for his secretary to retype and edit. Tom got into computer communications when he discovered that it would not only be simpler to transfer his drafts directly into his company's computer but that he could do this by phone while traveling. If Tom gets his drafts in early enough, he can review them "online" a day later to check his secretary's editing. Now many of Tom's reports are on his boss's desk before that welcome Friday night flight home. (Recently his wife learned how to leave messages for him in his "electronic mail box.")

Martha manages a team of technical writers. A demanding boss "pushed" her into computer communications because the company wanted manuals written and edited online so they could be easily transmitted via a communications network to their eight divisional offices. Martha soon learned that not only could she get feedback from these offices via electronic mail but that she could do most of her work without the necessity of shuffling paper between herself and her staff. The writers are all on the same communications network. In the several years that Martha has been online, enough new technical databases have been available to put the answers to the editorial staff's research needs as close as their keyboards.

Frank is a congressional aide who frequently roams the home district doing troubleshooting. He reports that using electronic mail services save him hours of playing telephone tag. They also lessen the problems of the 3 hour time difference between Washington and the West Coast. The office can keep a complete electronic file of all his transactions so that any follow up can be researched in a matter of minutes.

Walter manages a small investment company. In the last several years, he has been able to bypass expensive brokerage fees by doing his own research via computer communications combined with several analysis programs he purchased for his desktop machine. Most impressive is how his computer can put the stock market "wire" right in his home. He's now in the process of experimenting with an online brokerage service and soon will transfer all of his banking operations to a new computer-based service.

Micro-Mainframe Communications

As previously mentioned, your personal computer can act as a "dumb" terminal if properly equipped ("terminal emulator" mode or program) to communicate with your larger mini-or mainframe computer. But beyond this use, you may wish to transfer text or data between the systems. This is possible in many cases with the "communications software" described earlier. That is, you may wish to "download" data from a mainframe file into the cells of a "Lotus 1-2-3" spreadsheet, or from a text manuscript file into the word processing component of Ashton-Tate's "Framework." All such applications are possible if you have the required software, some of which may necessarily be available in the large machine as well as your personal computer.

Still, however, most personal computers cannot communicate fully with mini- or mainframe systems and this is an intense area of current development in the computer business. If you want the best compatibility between your desktop and larger computer systems, you might be advised to go computer shopping with this requirement in mind, rather than trying to retrofit. The larger computer companies—IBM, DEC, Wang—are increasingly responding to such needs.

Further Uses for You to Consider

Table 7.1 presents a brief summary of the many business or professional uses of personal computer communications. Again a number of the applications are discussed in more detail in Part Three of this book.

CREATE YOUR OWN ELECTRONIC BULLETIN BOARD OR MAIL SYSTEM

It is increasingly easy to use a personal computer as the "host" of your own communications system. This is a professional application of an "electronic bulletin board." Consider this professional example:

Karl, a recent management graduate, is in charge of personal computer implementation in the West Coast offices of a large national brokerage and diversified financial services firm. One of his greatest problems was that once he had computers installed on executives' desks, they often had questions about further uses of the programs they had learned, about new programs, or about the computers themselves. Because he could not be readily available for all of their calls, Karl established a "bulletin board" service, which was essentially one personal computer set aside in his office to receive, store, or send

Table 7.1. Applications of Personal Computer Communications

Banking ("Telebanking")

Surely you've seen ads for it already: "Write checks, shift funds among accounts, or check your balance from the keyboard of your home computer." Even if your local bank isn't yet offering these services, you can get them elsewhere. (See Chapter 11.)

Business Information

Want market quotes before they are published? How about the latest breaking news on stock offerings, corporate acquisitions, or even bankruptcies? You can not only get first-hand information about goings on in the business world, but background on any publicly listed company. (See Dow Jones New/Retrieval, in Chapter 12.)

Database Access ("Teleresearch")

Use the powerful computerized reference services that only technical libraries had a few years ago. Do research on the stock market. Put an electronic encyclopedia in your office. Gain access to large and valuable databases (see Chapter 12).

Mail or Conferencing ("Telemail")

Use "electronic mail" to send or receive messages from other subscribers on your information service whether they are a subscriber or not, have a letter sent to them in the next day's mail from the nearest post office by Western Union's EasyLink or MCI Mail (see Chapter 13). Several of the information utilities offer inexpensive "teleconference" services (see The Source and CompuServe, in Chapter 12).

Networking

Who else likes to chat about exotic travel, strange games, or is in love with their Apple computer? Join special interest group conversations; meet new friends; do professional networking.

Newsletters

Want the latest on winemaking, the inside information on cut-rate vacations? How about researching the computer software market? Over 175 special newsletters are now online via NewsNet (see Chapter 12).

News

Why wait for the newspaper to be delivered or some golden voiced announcer to read the headlines? Read them yourself with online news services. Read only what you want when you want it. Consult special news on sports or business.

Shopping

Go shopping from your keyboard. Look for discounts. Join a bartering service. Scan the classifieds or enter one yourself. See what's available in salvaged and damaged goods. Locate books, magazines, and tapes. (See Information Utilities, in Chapter 12.)

Table 7.1. (Continued)

Training ("Telelearning")

Locate schools and training services. Consider using online services to distribute training materials. Use constantly updated reference guides. Know how to access the world's most extensive bibliographies on any subject. (See Chapter 17.)

Travel

Have the latest airline guide as close as your computer. Or if you have your own plane, plan flight schedules. Make hotel, motel, or restaurant reservations. (See The Source, in Chapter 12.)

Weather

Are you flying across the country today? Will you need a raincoat or your jogging shorts tomorrow in Philadelphia? Get the weather forecast for anywhere, including ski areas.

---

messages. Users can call at any time and leave their questions. Once per day Karl logs on and leaves the answers. Recently, there have been two new developments. First, Karl now posts technical bulletins that reflect answers to questions most frequently posed by callers. Second, many users of the "board" find it handy for sending mail to one another. The system, now highly successful, cost less than $5000, including the cost of the host computer.

If your dealer cannot advise you on bulletin board software, consult a personal computer communications magazine (e.g., *Link-Up*) or try to locate board users in your local area. There are especially sophisticated programs available for the CP/M and MS-DOS operating systems for personal computers.*

---

*A very popular board program for the IBM, "RBBS-PC," is public domain software. Write to: Capital PC Users Group, P.O. Box 3189, Gaithersburg, MD 20878.

8
LOCAL AREA
NETWORKS

INTERCONNECTING ISLANDS OF INFORMATION

What Is a Local Area Network?

A local area network (LAN) is generally described as a private network that offers reliable high speed communications channels for connecting information processing equipment in usually but not necessarily a limited geographic area. This could be an office building or a complex of buildings that may include manufacturing operations or a college campus.

But you should not be misled by this apparently simple definition of what is an extremely important and useful tool for integrating the information flow in your office or factory. Some of its potential is illustrated in Figure 8.1.

Because the demand for telecommunications has kept pace or even leaped ahead of the adoption of computers in the office, on the factory floor, on the campus, or in the home, the development of new styles of LANs has been explosive. Telecommunications technology being what it is, LANs have become smaller and less complex while increasing the number of functions they can perform. So today we have LANs in a box, or components of the LAN built right into the computer or word processor, and you might very well have difficulty locating the "network" itself.

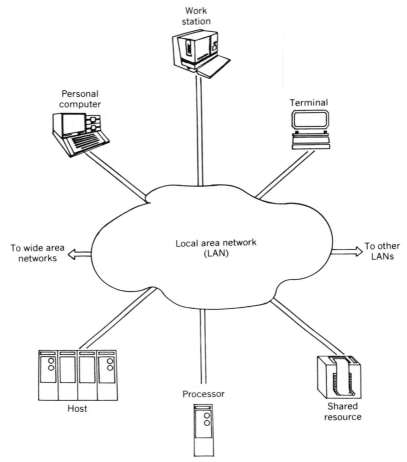

Figure 8.1. General concept of a LAN

What a Local Area Network Is Not

Don't confuse the LAN with the single cable running to the main-frame on which are usually connected several work stations, personal computers, printers, and possibly a data source. This is the traditional Input/Output Bus (I/O BUS).

Compare the I/O Bus in Figure 8.2 with the LAN in Figure 8.1. The Bus only permits data to be directly exchanged from processor to processor and to the mainframe. The I/O Bus usually connects components that are very dependent on each other and are part of a single system. In these systems, if one component fails, the entire

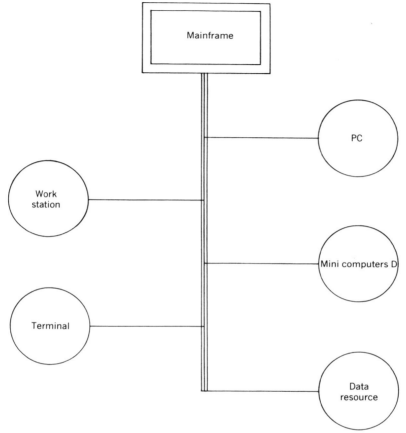

Figure 8.2.   An I/O is not a LAN

system is usually down for repairs. Because there are limited rules
of the road or protocols for shipping data around, I/O Bus systems
are usually easily overloaded and relatively slow. All of the information must be ''packaged'' in a similar fashion. That is, the messages are all of the same size and travel at the same speeds. This is
not always possible because your equipment will not operate at the
same speed nor use the same size messages. Because of these message size and speed requirements, all of the equipment on an I/O
Bus has to be designed to conform to the standards set by the mainframe computer to which the Bus is connected. Your ability to purchase equipment for your particular needs is often severely limited.

   With a LAN you can interconnect your islands of information

wherever they may be, in your office, on the factory floor, around your building, or even in your home as illustrated in Figure 8.1. Your LAN can be used for communications, data processing, office and factory automation, energy management and control, fire protection and security, teleconferencing, or television delivery.

WHAT CAN A LOCAL AREA NETWORK DO?

Local area networks are designed to:

Convert your tedious step-by-step office procedures into an efficient, continuous process capable of significant labor and time savings.

Provide relatively high speed data communications among your equipment, typically in the range of 1 to 10 megabits per second (for television you might want to go as high as 90 megabits per second).

Coordinate and manage operations that may be spread through more than one office, more than one building, and even across a city.

Operate and manage many independent devices, such as mainframes, minicomputers, personal computers, word processors, computer controlled machine tools and other factory and processing equipment that are computer controlled, telephones, facsimile and other document production equipment, electronic messaging equipment, television sets, teleconferencing bridges, security and energy control devices, electric typewriters, printers, and PBXs, for a starter.

Transmit information with as few errors as possible and with as few failures as possible at whatever speeds the equipment operates best.

Provide equal and immediate access to all equipment in your office or offices by all devices and equipment.

Grow gracefully as the business expands and new equipment "comes on line," and allow for new configurations as the need arises.

Be managed and maintained efficiently with limited staff.

Be inexpensive to construct and operate.

"Bypass" the local telephone carriers and go directly to another LAN across town or to the long distance network, thereby saving you communications dollars.

This last feature of a LAN is especially important these days. For example, you can purchase a LAN that interconnects personal computers and word processors located in several buildings, thereby reducing your need for the local telephone carrier's services, whose costs are likely to rise significantly over the next several years. Furthermore, you can assure yourself of immediate access to this transmission line because you control it. Should you want to use that connection for high speed data, or video as well as voice transmissions, you will not have to arrange with the carrier for special "preparation" of the transmission line. Since you control access to the transmission, you can ensure a high degree of security. Finally, and perhaps most important, you can design your LAN to enable you to increase the number of terminals to be interconnected as often and as gracefully as you wish.

HOW A LOCAL AREA NETWORK HELPS YOU MANAGE BETTER

Initially a LAN was simply a way for data processing systems to interconnect either through their own lines or the public switched telephone network, usually within one or more offices on one floor of a building. Almost all of the early systems were "hand made" or specially designed by offices using whatever interconnect equipment and software they needed to make it work. But as the number of different types of personal computers, word processors, electronic mail, and other systems proliferated, few if any being able to communicate with one another unless of the same make and manufacture, it became increasingly difficult for these local interconnect systems to work. Consequently, LANs were developed to serve specific needs and equipment.

Today the local networking concept has evolved to include a general purpose, multivendor system environment that provides interconnection for a variety of terminals and computers within one building or in several buildings, usually not more than a mile or so away. And it is no longer necessary to "package" your operations by manufacturer in order for them to work together. A well designed LAN will allow you to design your information flows to suit your business and your management style. Furthermore, you will be able to expand your operation just where it needs expansion, and if you manage the LAN properly with appropriately trained people, you will rarely have to worry about it. You can concentrate on managing the people and the information under your control.

Managers want to be able to plug their computers, printers, and other office equipment into each other just as they plug their lamps into an extension cord. If these devices were simply sending electrical impulses to each other it could be as easy as plugging lamps and electric typewriters into wall plugs and not being afraid of something blowing up. But it is not that simple. Local area networks must not only transmit the signals but must send them in a way that ensures that the information transmitted is understood. When you want the laser printer to print the document you just prepared, you do not want to see the dot-matrix printer working away. And if you "mail" a message from your communicating word processor to a word processor on the shipping room floor, you do not want the processor in the executive office to receive that message.

Local area networks provide both physical interconnection and software interconnection. What determines the cost of a LAN are the number of functions you wish it to perform, the variety of equipment to be interconnected, and the physical distribution of this equipment. The more functions, the more equipment, and the greater the distance between them, the higher the cost of the LAN.

The best way to understand just what a LAN can do for you is to examine its applications and how you use them to manage more efficiently. We do this in Table 8.1.

SOME EXAMPLES OF HOW LOCAL AREA NETWORKS WORK FOR MANAGERS

The One-Person Office

If you have purchased a personal computer, you probably have already installed and are operating with a simple LAN. Your home computer facility probably consists of a dot-matrix printer for the rough drafts, a letter quality printer, and a modem for accessing electronic mail and information services. Along with this equip-

Table 8.1. Managing Better with Local Area Networks

Local Area Network Applications	Management Benefits
Communications	
Communicates between equipment from many different manufacturers, makes communications between equipment transparent.	Gives you great flexibility in the purchase of equipment to suit you, and you do not have to worry about compatibility.
	Provides for message delivery and file transfer accurately, privately, and without delay.
	Creates an environment for easy interactive communications, across all levels of management.
	Reduces errors and misunderstandings that arise from misplaced paper.
	Saves time and money.
Data Processing	
Provides for distributed as well as stand-alone operation of computers, word processors, printers, typewriters, facsimile transmitters, multifunction work stations, PBXs, intelligent telephones, electronic mail and message systems, energy and fire control systems, etc.	Offers management control over how equipment is to be used. Provides for flexible utilization of equipment, centralized, decentralized, and distributed fashions.
	Provides for efficient allocation of employees to equipment, offline for trainees, online for experienced workers.
Provides for efficient utilization of a multiplicity of data processing resources. Unifies and integrates distributed components of a data processing system.	Makes available data processing as needed, thereby saving money and manpower.
	Enriches the information resources required for decision-making as needed.
	Calls on programs from all parts of the distributed system.
Office Automation	
Interconnects diverse word processing and peripheral equipment, such as printers, facsimile, and messaging equipment.	Provides for efficient time shared access to expensive equipment, saving money and time. Provides rapid, efficient, and secure transmission of files and documents.
	Ensures access to alternate equipment in case of individual failures, a fail safe availability.

Table 8.1. (Continued)

Local Area Network Applications	Management Benefits
	Adapts to variable speed of trained and skilled staff.
	Provides opportunity for efficient management of office operations and for increasing productivity.

Factory Automation

Local Area Network Applications	Management Benefits
Interconnects office information systems with manufacturing information systems.	Provides for integrated control and management of operations. Increases productivity by reducing time lags between office and factory floor. Reduces errors due to paper/people in data transmission from design to manufacture.
	Reduces inventories through tighter control of parts production.
	Introduces design changes more rapidly, thereby accelerating delivery of finished products.
	Reduces cost of management coordination.
	Prices final products more competitively.

Energy Management and Control

Local Area Network Applications	Management Benefits
LAN integrates energy management and control in a single reliable network.	Allows for area-wide control of energy from single control point for more immediate response to rapid changes in energy requirements.
	Conserves energy and reduces energy costs.

Fire Control and Security

Local Area Network Applications	Management Benefits
LAN integrates fire and security on a single reliable network.	Allows for centralized area-wide surveillance and more rapid response to emergencies.

Teleconferencing

Local Area Network Applications	Management Benefits
Interconnects intelligent telephones and teleconferencing bridges as well as video and graphic facilities, facsimile, and computers on a single network.	Provides for multimedia conferences throughout network area.
	Reduces cost of communications.
	Allows for rapid scheduling of important or emergency staff meetings.

ment came a number of accessories: an RS-232-C cable, a parallel adaptor board, a serial interface card, and serial port card. By following the instructions for connecting and installing these components, you installed your LAN for your home computer center. This LAN enables you to send documents to your dot-matrix or letter quality printer, and to your modem for telemailing. Your communicating software enables you to print the information you receive online, to store the information on your disks, or merely to read the incoming messages on your screen.

Note that your LAN is made up of both hardware and software, and your information flows as smoothly as if it were all in one piece of equipment.

Many LANs interconnect equipment that has been designed to be compatible and communicate at speeds low enough to be handled by the plain old telephone system (POTS). You can also transmit your information into your mainframe computer through the company's PBX. Once in your office where you have another personal computer and perhaps one or more communicating word processors and printers, you can access the information you stored in the main frame for office use. Your LAN now extends by way of POTS into yet another LAN in your office.

Automating the Department Office

Now consider an office with, say, a half-dozen personal computers, several printers including letter-quality and dot-matrix, and a plotter. There is a mainframe in the company, located in another building on the campus or industrial park.

This office is working with the telemarketing staff and has the primary responsibility for following up on the sales leads with formal quotes, responding to customers' letters, and keeping the warehouse and shipping department informed of stock and delivery requirements. The staff is managing information, sending and preparing messages to other personal computers and to the mainframe, preparing and sending correspondence to customers, maintaining weekly and daily schedules, and preparing monthly reports. To do so requires that the personal computers communicate with each other, access the printers, and store information in the company mainframe for the preparation of daily schedules, weekly reports, and monthly summaries. High speed communications (greater than what the public switched telephone systems can deliver) is necessary, as well as some form of traffic control among the personal computers so they do not all try to access printers at the same time.

This is an ideal example of the personal computer local area network or "PC LAN," a LAN specially designed for interconnecting personal computers with each other, with their peripherals, and to a mainframe. Communications among personal computers can be performed via a multiprocessor system into which all of the personal computers and their peripherals connect. These stand-alone "LANs-in-a-Box" are increasingly popular, especially if all of the personal computers are from the same manufacturer (even if different models); they provide physical interconnection and software compatibility. Indeed, new models of higher powered personal computers can be directly interconnected with as many as 25 personal computers of their own kind.

Our initial problem, communicating with the corporate mainframe, is solved either by a standard digitally switched PBX or by the voice/data PBX as discussed in Chapter 5. Modern PBXs, even if not the expensive voice/data PBXs, are increasingly digital, capable of switching data at speeds considerably greater than what most PC LANs require.

Personal computers with the added capability for interconnection may be several thousands of dollars more expensive than a "stand-alone" personal computer but you can save money by not having to purchase a LAN, in or out of a box. When you are interconnecting several dozen personal computers, printers, and modems across a good sized office, you will require either a number of LANs-in-a-Box or multiprocessors. Or you may go the next step and purchase a distributed LAN, one for which you may be paying by the foot or mile. We shall have more to say about the cost of these installations.

Figure 8.3 is a good example of how you can use a LAN creatively to transform an overloaded paper office into an automated one.

If your office is like many offices it is probably clogged with paper and delays. Five related tasks, information processing, preparation, dissemination, storage, and computation, are performed independently of one another, or so it seems, as paper waits for people or for more paper. Compare your piecework office with a "continuous process" office on a LAN in Figure 8.3.

The preparation and a portion of the dissemination tasks are in-

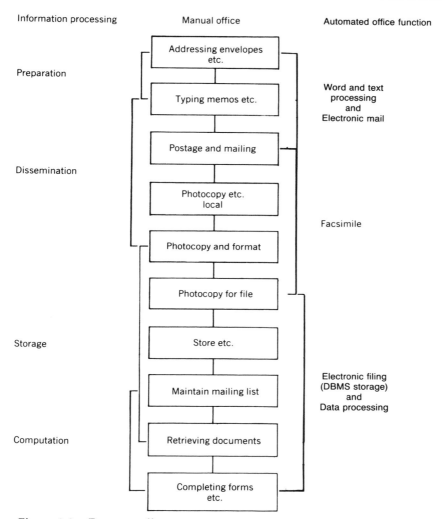

Figure 8.3. From an office parts operation to an office process operation

tegrated into a single operation by putting word and text processing systems "online" ready for electronic mail delivery. The pos-
tage and mailing tasks are eliminated entirely. Instead of
photocopying for local distribution the electronic mail network distributes the information to all parties who are to be copied for the
messages and texts. Electronically mailed documents are transmitted to facsimile (FAX) stations where the documents are then delivered to parties not on the electronic mail network. Documents that

are not required in the form of "hard copy" are transmitted directly
from the mail network to the electronic data base management storage, while those that require "hard copy" are filed in the traditional manner or reduced for micrographic storage. Mailing lists
and documents are listed for later retrieval, necessary forms completed with necessary calculations using the data delivered to the
computers directly from the word and text processing station via
electronic mail.

Automating Office to Factory Operations

Consider an automated office engaged in engineering design and
manufacturing operation. Generally engineers and designers are
not located on the factory floor. Manufacture and assembly operations are typically separated from design and engineering depart-
ments either in another building of the facility or even some distance away, perhaps in another city. While manufacture and
assembly operations have their own foreman with their information needs, engineering managers are responsible for seeing that
design changes are expeditiously carried out and that quality control specifications are altered accordingly. Personal computers and
other intelligent terminals are on the floor to inform the manufacturing and assembly managers of changes to be implemented rapidly. In fully automated production operations design changes as
well as quality control adjustments are transmitted directly from
the engineering office to the machines and testing devices in the
factory. Note that the ability to directly coordinate the operations
of the equipment in the factory by way of the LAN can reduce labor.

In the factory and engineering offices there are usually a number
of different devices, for example, several models of personal computers and data terminals, plotters and computer aided design terminals, computer controlled automatic test equipment and assembly systems. They operate at many different speeds and codes. They
are not compatible with one another; you cannot just plug them
into one another and expect them to work properly or at all. Furthermore, the distance between the engineering office and the factory is typically somewhat more than a mile. New remote assembly
areas may be established and the number of equipment to be interconnected is likely to grow to well over 100, scattered more than 2
miles from the executive engineering offices.

If your firm had multiplant operations in several cities, these are likely to be interconnected by their own LANs much as the plant previously described is linked by a LAN. Provisions can be made for these LANs to interconnect by way of the private switched packet networks, such as Telenet or Tymenet. Suitable protocols (such as X.25) are provided by the LAN to enable computers in one city to access terminals on production lines, or in offices in other cities, or even to control machines on factory floors in distant cities.

Clearly this is a job for one of the more advanced LAN installations. They must not only provide for efficient physical interconnection but also establish rules of the road or protocols for the information being transmitted. This ensures that information is rapidly available, at the right place at the right speed, and in a language that the machine can understand.

The Multi-purpose Automated Facility

Up to this point we have been describing LANs that are used primarily for the management of information, and this information has been in the form of bits and bytes. As plant operations become more distributed you want to take advantage of the ability of information technology to reduce the cost of coordinating these scattered operations. To do so you need to take advantage of all forms of communications, voice and video as well as data. Also you want to do more than just communicate. For example, with distributed factory operations, you may want to enhance plant security and control energy in order to reduce costs. Video surveillance and alarm systems can be installed in warehouses and offices throughout your facility. All of this can be done on a LAN. The more you want to integrate your operations the more important and expensive the LAN becomes. Furthermore, the more specialized your functions become, the more likely you will need a specially designed system, one that requires operation, maintenance, and training of your personnel. We discuss these issues subsequently but first, do you need a LAN and if so, what kind?

DO YOU NEED A LOCAL AREA NETWORK?

We do not assume that all firms have mainframe computers through which their staffs can communicate or that data is being sent through a PBX. However, with the growing use of personal computers in offices and increasing use and dependence on data in the office, it is very likely that you will want more rapid and more accurate communications between these computers and word processors. You might also want to send this data to other offices over the telephone, or even to the factory or shipping floor. Most managers will not want to spend their time or the time of their staff ''hacking away'' with their computers and word processors to get them to talk to one another. But not everyone will need a LAN to avoid this task despite what the advertisements tell you.

If your operations are larger than a one-person office or small office, say with more than 10 personal computers, work stations, and other communicating terminals or printers, you will very likely want to consider a LAN. Unless you are an engineer looking for some design excitement or have that person among your employees you will need a consultant to design the system. But before you run off and hire that person, you need to determine just what you need. You should carefully and completely specify the system you want. You will find that answering these questions is an exercise in the corporate strategic planning of your firm's future. We noted earlier that telecommunications is becoming an important strategic resource, and so it is.

Here are five questions you should ask before calling in the consultant:

1.   What Functions will Your LAN Perform?

Will you be communicating with voice, data, image, or a combination of these?

Will you require electronic messaging between your office and other offices or to some external facility?

Do you prepare major documents for distribution among different equipment including printers and facsimile equipment?

Will you be accessing remote mainframe computers?

Are you planning to engage in teleconferencing?

Will you be communicating with computer aided design or computer aided manufacturing equipment?

What are your communication requirements for security?

What are your energy control requirements?

2. What Are the Traffic Requirements of Your System?

    How do you want the information to flow among your equipment?

    What are your priority information flows?

    What is your transaction traffic in your facility?

    How much of a delay in traffic flow can you tolerate?

3. What Are the Reliability Requirements for Your System?

    Specify reliability requirements for each of the functions of your system:

    Transfers of files

    Database inquiries

    Voice communications

    Data transmission

    Energy control and management

    Security

    How much downtime can you tolerate in each of these areas?

    Do you want to centralize or decentralize the network control equipment?

4. How do You Propose to Perform Maintenance on the System?

    Will you maintain the system yourself or will you depend on maintenance of software and hardware provided by the system designer/supplier?

    Who will be responsible for monitoring the performance of your LAN?

5. What Are the Likely System Growth Requirements?

    What equipment do you expect will be added?

    What new types of traffic are anticipated?

    How will the initial traffic patterns likely change over time?

    Do you expect that the location of the equipment will be changed over time?

Table 8.2 will help you keep track of your findings and develop the specifications to which your consultant should design. (It will also

Table 8.2. *Do You Need a Local Area Network?—A Checklist*

	Part I—Functional Requirements							
	Cost	Control	Access	Reliability	Security	Growth	Location[a]	Cost
Information management								
Communications								
Voice								
Electronic mail								
Teleconferencing								
Data processing								
Office automation								
Factory automation								
Energy management and control								
Fire and security								
Micrographics equipment								
Intelligent telephones								
Business graphics								
CAD/CAM equipment								

[a]Location: Single office; multiple offices, that is in one building, within a square mile, beyond one square mile.

Table 8.2. (Continued)

Part II—Inventory of Equipment and Systems

Variety, Number and Location
of Equipment

	Number	Message Format (Word Length)	Data Rate (Bits/second)
Personal computers			
Model No.			
Model No.			
Model No.			
Minicomputers			
Model No.			
Model No.			
Model No.			
Mainframe computers			
Model No.			
Model No.			
Printers			
Model No.			
Model No.			
Model No.			
Word processors (without modem)			
Model No.			
Model No.			
Model No.			
Word processors (with modem)			
Model No.			
Model No.			
Model No.			
Fax equipment			
Professional work stations			
Multifunction work stations			

confirm your need for a LAN.) For example, the first question asks you to specify the functions your LAN is to perform: information management by voice, electronic mail, or teleconferencing. You want control over the network that is distributing this information, but you may want to limit access to that network. Further, you demand very high reliability and security, and your planning has determined that the number of people accessing the voice communications network will likely double over the next 5 years as will the users of electronic mail. You expect, however, that the single teleconferencing room you have planned for and the number of offices accessing that network will very likely remain the same. Finally, you note in the final column that your staff will probably grow to occupy several offices in your own building and another office in an adjacent building, across the street. The cost column is for the consultant to fill in. This arrangement of critical information enables you to weigh the cost of what you want against its value to your firm.

Your design consultant will want to have information about the likely equipment you will be using and something about the nature of the messages you are likely to be sending, in short, the information on Table 8.2. You may not have all of this information at your fingertips, but if you have a good idea of the types of the equipment you will be using (generally similar to what you are using now) you can ask your supplier or the consultant to help you with the details of the model number, word length, and so on.

ACQUIRING YOUR LAN

Today, technical journals report at least 75 vendors offering LANs to suit a wide range of network requirements. A listing of some of these vendors is provided in Table 8.3. But almost every week a new vendor is likely to be offering features that may be more suitable to your specific needs.

There are two ways for you to obtain your LAN:

1. If you are a one-person or small office engaged in communications and with, say, a dozen personal computers of the same type and manufacturer with associated peripherals that are compatible, you can almost always purchase a LAN-in-a-Box or a multiprocessor that will do what you want. You may want to add security precautions in the form of special software, also available from the providers of the LAN. Will your system be available only to your staff or will customers or clients have access? Will your staff be servicing and programming the network? Clearly, it makes a difference if the system is to be available to outsiders as well as your staff. The system provider can suggest physical measures, many of which you may already be using, such as intrusion alarms and smoke and heat detectors. There are also controlled passwords and

Table 8.3. A Partial Listing of the Major LAN Vendors

Supplier	Network	Applications
A.B. Dick Company 5700 West Toughy Avenue Chicago, IL 60648 (312) 763-1900	The Loop	General business Electronic mail Word processing
Altos Computer Systems 2360 Bering Drive San Jose, CA 95131 (408) 946-6700	Altos-Net	General business Electronic mail Word processing
Amtel Systems Corporation 1293 Anviwood Avenue Sunnyvale, CA 94086 (408) 734-5092	Messenger	General business Industrial
Apollo Computer Inc. 15 Elizabeth Drive Chelmsford, MA 01824 (617) 256-6600	DOMAIN	Industrial Other
Apple Computer, Inc. 20525 Mariani Avenue Cupertino, CA 95014 (408) 973-3019	AppleNet	General business Other
Concord Data Systems 303 Bear Hill Road Waltham MA 02154 (617) 890-1394	Token/Net	General business Electronic mail Word processing Industrial Other
Covus Systems 2090 O'Toole Avenue San Jose, CA 95131 (408) 946-7700	Omninet Appleshare	Industrial Other
Datapoint 9725 Datapoint Drive San Antonio, TX (512) 699-7059	ARCNET	General business Electronic mail Word processing Industrial Other
Digital Equipment 129 Parker Street Maynard, MA 10754 (617) 493-4097	Ethernet	Electronic mail Industrial Other
Digital Microsystems 1755 Embarcadero Oakland, CA 94606 (415) 532-3686	HiNet	General business Electronic mail Word processing Industrial Other

Table 8.3. (Continued)

Supplier	Network	Applications
Gandalf Data 33 John Street Manotick, Ontario, Canada (613) 596-3841	PACXNET	General business Word processing Industrial Other
Intecom 601 Intelcom Drive Allen, TX 75002 (313) 973-1500	LANmark	General business Electronic mail Word processing Industrial Other
IBM 1133 Westchester Avenue White Plains, NY 10604 (914) 238-2000	Series/1 Ring	General business Industrial Other
Intersil Systems 1275 Hammerwood Avenue Sunnyvale, CA 94086 (408) 743-4300	GEnet	General business Electronic mail Word processing Industrial Other
Logica 666 Third Avenue New York, NY 10017 (212) 599-0828	Polynet	General business Electronic mail Word processing Industrial Other
Network Systems 7600 Boone Avenue North Brooklyn Park, Minneapolis, MN 55428 (612) 425-2202	HYPERchannel	General business Industrial Other
Prime Computer Prime Park Natick, MA 01760 (617) 655-8000	Ringnet	General business Electronic mail Word processing Industrial Other
Starnet Data Systems 1331 West Evans Avenue Denver, CO 80223 (303) 935-3566	Starnet II	General business Electronic mail Word processing Industrial Other
Three Rivers 720 Gross Avenue Pittsburgh, PA 15224 (412) 621-6250	Ethernet	General business Electronic mail Word processing Other

Table 8.3. (Continued)

Supplier	Network	Applications
Ungermann-Bass 2560 Mission College Boulevard Santa Clara, CA 95050 (408) 496-0111	Net/One Baseband Net/One Broadband	General business Electronic mail Word processing Industrial Other
Wang Laboratories One Industrial Avenue Lowell, MA 01851 (617) 459-5000	Wangnet	General business Electronic mail Word processing Other
Xerox 1341 West Mockingbird Lane Dallas, TX 75247 (313) 536-9129	Ethernet	General business Word processing Other
Zilog 1315 Dell Avenue Campbell, CA 95008 (408) 370-8000	UNET	General business Word processing

other authorization codes that can be assigned to your personnel. But in all cases, the effectiveness of any security is determined by how well you manage the security procedures you adopt.

2. If you are a multioffice or multiplant operation you may wish to seek the advice of consultants who can route you to the most appropriate LAN provider. You are likely to find that if your needs are rather extensive, you will want to have your own staff manage and maintain your LAN. The world of the LAN is so relatively new and changing so rapidly as new telecommunications options emerge from the competitive marketplace, you may be making a considerable investment in engineering staff. Your management skills will be tested to ensure that they do not provide you with more than you need. That can be very expensive.

HOW MUCH WILL IT COST?

The cost of your LAN will depend on:
1. The functions you wish to perform
2. The number of equipment you are interconnecting
3. The distribution of this equipment.

A guide to LAN costs is given in Table 8.4.

Table 8.4. Quick Guide to LAN Costs

Type of LAN	Approximate Cost
LAN-in-a-Box	Under $1000
LAN via PBX	Cost imbedded in PBX functions (See Chapter 5 on PBXs)
Intra/Inter-office LAN interconnected by:	$300 to $500 per network connection
Twisted pair	$ .40–$2.25 per foot
Coaxial cable	$2.50–$4.00 per foot
Fiber optic cable	$2.00–$7.00 per foot

MANAGING YOUR LOCAL AREA NETWORK

Because your valuable and private information will be transmitted among widely distributed equipment across many offices in many buildings and even in several cities, security will be one of your major concerns. You must plan for security through system design as well as training. Security can be designed into every mode or at every connection in your network. Access to critical terminals can be limited by office practices and monitoring. Additionally, certain software protocols, such as passwords, must be created. Your staff must be trained to respect and support these security procedures.

The more wide-ranging your LAN and the more functions it performs, the greater will be the need for maintenance. Often a maintenance contract can be negotiated with the supplier or installer of the network. But in the long run, you will probably want to have your own staff monitor and maintain the network. Experienced telephone technicians are usually best qualified to do these tasks and you will rarely require additional design engineering once the system has been installed, especially if you have carefully planned for system growth. This is one of the features of a well planned and designed LAN. A good technician will ensure system performance so that you will be able to use the system even if some equipment may be temporarily offline for maintenance and repair. Don't overlook the possibility of upgrading one of your own maintenance people; many LAN providers offer programs for training technicians for their systems.

Training yourself and your staff in order to get the most out of your LAN investment cannot be an afterthought. Training is a very cost-effective investment and ensures the maximal use of your system.

9

MOBILE PHONES AND PAGING: TRANSFORMING TRAVEL TIME TO PRODUCTIVE TIME

THE COMMUNICATING EXECUTIVE

Mobile telephone services make it possible for you to be in many places at the same time, no matter how your staff and offices are distributed. Even with your employees on the move they can contact you and you can contact them, not only for emergencies but when a quick decision will give you the competitive edge needed to capture a contract or close negotiations to your advantage. And when you are stuck in traffic between calls, your next appointment need not be kept waiting and fuming; you can call and report your dilemma, even begin your conversation while parked on what you often think is the world's biggest parking lot. In short, you can transform your staff's and your travel time into productive time.

Mobile communications has become the fastest growing telecommunications industry in the United States and in the world. Many of today's executives know exactly why this is so. Long trips to work, almost always in the privacy of your automobile when you are thinking about the day ahead, generate the need to communicate your thoughts before they fly out of your head, and you can't stop to write them down. You want to start your staff working on some of these ideas as soon as possible. You want to set up the meeting that grew out of your evening's "home work" before the participants run off for their day's work and set up their own schedules.

THE MANY OPTIONS FOR MOBILE COMMUNICATIONS

The communications revolution offers many choices that enable you to transform travel time into productive time. Several mobile communication options have been available for some time. Obstetricians and plumbers wore pagers strapped to their belts that beeped at the wrong time, often interrupting our concentration at the movies or at a concert. Police officers, firefighters, Hollywood executives, and politicians had radio telephones in their automobiles. And taxis and delivery vans often were equipped with radio dispatch systems in order to get them to their clients faster. But there was always a greater demand for mobile communications than there were radio frequencies and users constantly complained of time spent waiting to get on the air.

The telecommunications revolution has changed all that. The radio spectrum is still a scarce resource, but we know how to utilize it better. Now we are so good at it that we can use the radio almost as we use a telephone. Table 9.1 is a quick guide to these choices.

CELLULAR MOBILE TELEPHONE SYSTEMS

The popular phrase today in mobile communications is ''cellular mobile telephone systems.'' Figure 9.1 illustrates a cellular network and its operations.

Bell Laboratories came up with the idea of using many transmitters to serve small areas, for example, areas with a radius of less than 10 miles. To each of these areas or cells is assigned a frequency or channel in a manner to ensure that there is no interference between cells. Note in our Figure 9.1 how the pattern of frequency assignments is arranged so that cells with the same frequency are not close to one another. As a motorist drives along, the receiver in the cell nearest to the caller's vehicle picks up the call and relays it to the area mobile telephone switching office. There a computer switches the call to the appropriate local telephone office if the called party is at a stationary telephone or to a receiver in another cell if the called party is on another mobile phone. When the motorist goes from one cell to another along the street the call is passed from one cell to another with no noticeable fading. Because frequencies are separated from each other as we show in the figure you can use the same frequency over and over again just as television stations

Table 9.1. Mobile Communications at a Glance

What It Does	How It Helps You Manage	Advantages	Disadvantages
Paging System			
Sends "beeps" or vibrations to roving users to tell receiver to call paging operator.	In emergencies locates key person for new instructions, insures that you are always "on call" and in control.	Small, personal receiver, low cost wide-area range, easy to purchase and install.	One-way, inhuman, limited information transfer, long wait times for caller. Some people resent invasion of privacy.
Dispatch System			
Transmits short messages to vehicles on road, through dispatcher.	Sends instructions and important information to staff on road. Keeps you always in control.	You own, operate, and control system. Can be used where there are no telephones.	Single channel for send and receive. No privacy, no direct contact between you and employee. Limited range.
Radio Telephone System (IMTS)			
Calls sent and received through public telephone system.	Provides all benefits of your telephone while traveling. You are never out of touch or control.	Multiple switched channels reduce wait time. More privacy. Can be used where there is no wired telephone.	Long wait time, limited range, interference. Difficult to obtain.
Citizen's Band System			
Party line for many users. Your conversations can be heard by everyone.	Can be used in a pinch for signaling staff if message is veiled.	Low cost, easy to obtain, and easy to use.	No privacy, limited range. Rarely used for business.

Table 9.1. (Continued)

What It Does	How It Helps You Manage	Advantages	Disadvantages
Cellular Mobile Telephone System			
Calls sent and received through public telephone system as in radio telephone system.	Provides all benefits of your intelligent telephone while traveling in auto, air, or train. Can be used as a fixed telephone to bypass local loop.	No waiting times, can be fully private, no fading, nationwide, worldwide coverage soon. Data transmission coming but limited. Satellite access. Can bypass local carrier. Units can sometimes operate on IMTS.	Expensive but costs falling. Not yet in every city.
Packet Radio System			
Designed for computer-to-computer communications	Access information utilities with your "lap" personal computer from wherever you may be.	Low cost transmission, no waiting, privacy, high speed use. Satellite access.	Not yet fully available, high cost equipment for a time.

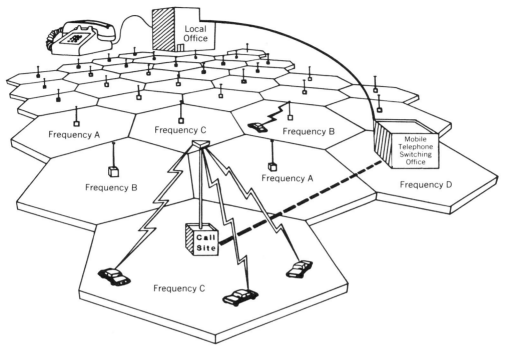

Frequency A

Frequency C

Frequency B

Local Office

Mobile Telephone Switching Office

Frequency B

Frequency A

Frequency D

Call Site

Frequency C

Figure 9.1. How cellular mobile telephone systems work.

in different cities use the same frequency without interfering with each other. If the number of users in an area or even in a cell gets so large that users get busy signals, the cells can be subdivided again into smaller cells and the same frequencies used again in the new cells, keeping in mind the proper separations to avoid interference.

Cellular systems are expensive. The black box in your car and the portable phone itself can cost in the neighborhood of $2000 or more. However, experts say that within the next four to five years equipment prices will fall to between $700 and $1000. In most systems you pay as much as $40 per month access fee and a rate of 27 cents to 45 cents for each minute whenever a call is made or received. And to this you must add any long distance and other charges for call forwarding, voice mail, and other intelligent telephone services you may incur to reach your party. The average user is paying about $150 per month, but this varies from city to city by as much as 20 percent either way. Industry observers predict that as more companies get into the business, operating costs could be cut by as much as 50 percent. However, cost is likely to take a back seat to need and convenience, if your business and your management style require being in control at all times no matter where you may be or when.

HELP FOR THE MANAGER ON THE RUN

When you talk to your colleagues who have caught the mobile phone bug you are likely to hear such glowing comments as "I don't know how I got along without one all of these years" or "I couldn't operate my business without it now." The following are two examples that might explain their enthusiasm.

Managing a Fast Moving Consulting Firm

You manage a small consulting company with a staff of five, four roving consultants, a secretary–receptionist (and sometime dispatcher). Long ago you found that your consulting staff likes to work out of their home offices and rarely do more than two of them come into the main office at the same time. Monthly staff meetings are often held at your favorite restaurant. It's clear that much of your consulting is performed on the client's premises and report writing is homework for your staff. Do you need your suite of three offices and reception area?

Much of your own time is spent visiting prospective clients or regular clients that have called for you. Now and then you wish you could call in a member of your staff who really can deal with this client's problem. You usually handle this by setting up a meeting for that expert for the next day, keeping your fingers crossed that your staff consultant will be available and the lost day will not turn your client off.

How much would it cost to outfit your consultants with their own cellular mobile phones? Compare this with the rental cost of your office. What if you gave up the two offices and just kept your office as a conference room/office leaving the secretary-dispatcher as is. It might surprise you to discover that within a year or less you will have recovered the cost of your mobile phone system capital investment, your clients will be impressed with how quickly you can respond to their calls, and you are pleased at how many more tasks your staff can undertake. You call on more prospects than before as your secretary catches you in your car between calls.

Think of all the businesses that are similar. Salespersons can follow up more leads without having to return to their office. Real estate brokers could make more house calls and not miss that prospect who gets the urge to visit the property just one more time. (One real estate executive claims that there is a 50 percent increase in his agents' productivity since he outfitted them with cellular mobile telephones.) How often have you seen salespersons hunting for a public phone while out on the road calling to inquire if a certain client wants to close a deal or would like a visit?

Cost recovery time may not be as important to you as are other trade-offs. For example, the real estate agents themselves might want to invest in the mobile phone if they think it will bring them sales, or the firm might want to share the cost by paying a portion of their monthly phone charges. Office space isn't the only place where money is saved or made; there are the satisfied customers, too.

Cash Management on the Run

Consider the case of Robert, the controller of a midsized microprocessor firm supplying microcomputer and office automation product manufacturers. Robert knows that in today's highly volatile money market, it's electronic money or information about money that makes money. Things move fast, and for Robert to make the best use of his money he has to know almost to the hour how much his money is worth and how much it costs to get new money. And he needs to have an up-to-the-minute cash and sales position of his firm when he is negotiating for money. Although he pays his bank for this information, which usually reaches him on his office terminal, what if he is not in the office?

He could ask his secretary to call on the bank's computer for him, and call him at some prearranged number where she could read off the important figures. Not exactly the best solution. Robert is paying for (but not using!) an interactive inquiry service which accesses the bank's decision-making program. The cellular mobile phone can come to the rescue, only this time with Robert's portable computer and a modem. No matter where Robert is he can call into the bank's computer and interact with the data so crucial to his firm.

WHERE IS THE PAYOFF FOR THE MANAGER?

If you manage a sales operation, selling products or services, the big payoff in your firm's or department's use of telecommunications is in the areas that directly link you to your customer throughout the entire marketing cycle. The sooner your staff can deliver the appropriate product or service information, the more rapidly they can prepare the cost estimates and proposals and the sooner they can close the deal.

For any manager who wants to be effective, keeping in touch, being available when needed, must rank high on his or her agenda. While you cannot always be available in person, you can be contacted wherever you might be to provide that all-important assurance by the chief executive the client wants. In short, you are **always there!**

HOW PRIVATE ARE CELLULAR MOBILE PHONE SYSTEMS?

We have just heard the good news about cellular phone systems; now to the bad news. Cellular mobile transmissions are radio transmissions and if someone wants to listen in, it's relatively easy to do so. People listen in on police and fire radio telephone conversations and, indeed, receivers are sold for just that purpose. There is a growing hobby in monitoring cellular mobile conversations. The public's desire to eavesdrop has created a rather substantial market in scanners, radio receivers that can tune across the entire range of frequencies used by cellular transmitters. It is not easy to follow a cellular mobile conversation that may change its frequency as often as the speakers cross cell boundaries. Even though the antibugging laws for wired telephones are being applied to cellular mobile services, you should be aware that you might be "bugged."

HOW TO OBTAIN YOUR CELLULAR MOBILE TELEPHONE SERVICES

What's Available in the Marketplace?

Cellular transmission services are common carrier services whose rates are regulated by the state utility commissions. The FCC has divided up the country into 90 cellular mobile telephone service regions, and has so far allocated these regions to just two carriers in each region. One of these systems can be owned and operated by the Regional Bell Operating Company (often referred to as an RBOC), the holding company that owns the telephone carrier company that delivers your telephone services. The cellular mobile company owned by the RBOC is referred to as a "wireline carrier." The other cellular mobile company can be owned and operated to a "nonwireline carrier."

There are seven Bell Cellular Mobile Telephone companies in the nation, one in each of the seven regional telephone holding companies (the RBOCs) the divestiture set up. In addition there are the nonwireline carriers that are operating in these regions. The wireline and nonwireline carriers in the top 30 markets are shown in Table 9.2. In Chicago, for example, the wireline provider is Ameritech Mobile, while the nonwireline carrier is Rogers Radio Communications, Inc. In Los Angeles, the wireline carrier is PacTel Mobile Access and the nonwireline carrier is the Los Angeles Cellular Corporation. Note in Table 9.2 that not all of the nonwireline cellular carriers are listed. The reason for this is that these carriers may be a bit behind the RBOCs in getting into business; they had to outbid others for the franchise and that took time.

Making Your Purchase

Selecting your car phone is your prime concern, since the dealer is probably an agent of a specific carrier and will also arrange for your access to the appropriate cellular carrier. Cellular phones are new to the market. There are more than three dozen different brands on the market and many more dealers, agents, and resellers who can provide you with a phone. For example, in each of the Los Angeles, Milwaukee, Minneapolis, and Washington/Baltimore markets, more than 30 agents, resellers, and dealers are competing for your business. Acquiring the right phone, either leasing or purchasing the services, requires planning and smart shopping.

In Table 9.3 we list some of the cellular suppliers who are providing cellular phones under their own label to the marketplace.

Here are some questions you should ask when you select your mobile cellular phone:

1. *How Important Is the Manufacturer's Reputation to You?* If this is important to you, find out how long the dealer has been manu-

Table 9.2. Cellular Network Operators in the Top 30 Markets

Cellular Geographic Service Area	Wireline Operator	Nonwireline Operator
NYC/Nassau-Suffolk/ Newark/ Patterson-Clifton/ Passaic/ Jersey City	NYNEX Mobile	Cellular Telephone
Los Angeles/Long Beach/ San Bernardino/Anaheim/ Santa Ana-Garden Grove/ Riverside/ Ontario	PacTel Mobile Access	Los Angeles Cellular Corporation
Chicago	Ameritech Mobile	Rogers Radio Communications, Inc.
Philadelphia	Bell Atlantic Mobile Systems	Automatic Cellular Systems, Inc.
Detroit/Ann Arbor	Ameritech Mobile	Detroit Cellular Telco
Boston/Lowell/Brockton/ Lawrence/Haverill	NYNEX Mobile	Yankee Celltel
San Francisco/Oakland	GTE Mobilnet	—
Washington, D.C./ Maryland/ Virginia	Bell Atlantic Mobile Systems	Washington-Baltimore Cellular Telephone Co.
Dallas/Ft. Worth	Southwestern Bell Mobile Systems	D/FW Signal Co.
Houston	GTE Mobilnet	Houston Cellular Tel. Co.
St. Louis/Illinois	Southwestern Bell Mobile Services	Cybertel
Miami/Ft. Lauderdale/ Hollywood	Bell South Mobile Services	—
Pittsburgh	Bell Atlantic Mobile Systems	MCI Cellular Telephone
Baltimore	Bell Atlantic Mobile Systems	American Teleservices
Minneapolis/St. Paul/ Wisconsin	New Vector Communications, Inc.	MCI/Cellcom
Cleveland	GTE Mobilnet	North Ohio Cellular
Atlanta	Bell South Mobile Services	Gen-Cell.
San Diego	PacTel Mobile Access	—
Denver/Boulder	New Vector Communications, Inc.	—
Seattle/Everett	New Vector Communications, Inc.	Interstate Mobile, Inc.

Table 9.2.   (Continued)

Cellular Geographic Service Area	Wireline Operator	Nonwireline Operator
Milwaukee	Ameritech Mobile	Milwaukee Telco
Tampa/St. Petersburg	GTE Mobilnet	
Cincinnati/Kentucky/ Indiana	Ameritech Mobile	South Ohio Telco
Kansas City, Missouri– Kansas	Southwestern Bell Mobile Services	—
Buffalo	NYNEX Mobile	Buffalo Telephone Co.
Phoenix	New Vector Commu- nications, Inc.	Metromobile
San Jose, California	GTE Mobilnet	—
Indianapolis	GTE Mobilnet	Indianapolis Telco
New Orleans	Bell South Mobile Ser- vices	—
Portland, Oregon/ Washington	GTE Mobilnet	Interstate Mobile

facturing mobile equipment. Remember, however, that the many newcomers without long established reputations in mobile radio equipment may provide equipment that works just as well and might cost a bit less than the equipment from the more established manufacturers. Perhaps what's more important is making sure you can obtain repair service when needed. If you are now using a paging system or old style radio telephone you may be able to make an attractive arrangement with your provider for the new equipment and, further, you already know how reliable that provider is.

2. *Is Price Important to You?*   All cellular phones are required to meet certain minimum FCC requirements. What you often pay for on the more expensive deluxe models are features you may not really need.

3. *How Often Will You Be Using the Phone?*   If you are going to make frequent use of the phone (if you are the telephone personality that feels out of place without the telephone at your ear), then you might consider some special features, such as a hands free speaker phone. It will probably be safer, too, since you can drive while talking and not take your hands off the wheel.

AT&T Technologies, Inc.
3800 Golf Road
Rolling Meadows, IL 60008
(312) 981-2798

CTI, Inc.
P.O. Box 71, Highway 45, South
Corinth, MI 38834
(601) 287-8081

Ericsson Communications
Cellular Systems Marketing
1290 Wall Street, West
Lyndhurst, NJ 07071
(201) 460-8030

E.F. Johnson Company
299 Johnson Avenue
Waseca, MN 56093
(507) 835-6222

GTE Communication Systems
Dept. 582/A6
400 North Wolf Road
Northlake, IL 60164
(312) 681-7100

Fujitsu America, Inc.
10 East 53rd Street
New York, NY 10022
(212) 308-7920

General Electric Company
Mountain View Road
Lynchburg, VA 24502
(804) 528-7450

Motorola Communications &
Electronics, Inc.
1301 E. Algonquin Road, SH-4
Schaumberg, IL 60196
(312) 576-7758

NEC America, Inc.
Mobile Radio Division
4936 West Rosecrans Avenue
Hawthorne, CA 90250
(213) 973-2071

Mitsubishi International
1098 N. Tower Lane
Bensenville, IL 60106
(312) 595-6494

Tectel Systems, Inc.
Country Club Road
Meadow Lands, PA 15347
(412) 228-6476

Harris Corp. RF Comm. Group
1680 University Avenue
Rochester, NY 14610
(716) 244-5830

Hitachi America, Ltd.
2990 Gateway Dr., Suite 1000
Norcross, GA 30071
(404) 446-8820

ITT Telecom
3100 Highwoods Blvd.
Raleigh, NC 27604
(919) 872-3359

Kokusai Electronic Co. Ltd.
El Segundo, CA 90245
(800) 421-5702

Northern Telcom, Inc.
1201 East Arapaho Road
Richardson, TX 75081
(214) 234-7896

NovAtel Communications
2820 Peterson Place
Norcross, GA 30071
(404) 449-6666

OKI Advanced Communications
1 University Place
Hackensack, NJ 07601
(201) 348-7933

Panasonic Industrial Company
Telecommunications Division
1 Panasonic Way
Secaucas, NJ 07094
(201) 348-7933

Quintron Corporation
1 Quintron Way
P.O. Box 3726
Quincy, IL 62305
(217) 223-3211

Stromberg-Carlson
400 Rinehart Road
Lake Mary, FL 32746
(305) 849-4900

4. *Are You Buying or Leasing a Phone for a New Car or for a Car You Already Own?* Installation is critical to the efficient operation of the system, so if it is a new car, arrange for the car dealer to install the phone. If for an old car, you might shop around for the best installation price. Check with your colleagues who are using cellular phones.

5. *How Long do You Plan to Keep Your Car?* If you are planning to sell the car relatively soon, ensure that the phone can be easily moved to your new car and know how much it will cost. Sometimes the auto dealer will do the job at no extra charge when you purchase your new car.

6. *Do You Need a Phone that You Can Carry with You in Addition to Use in Your Car?* You will not be spending all of your time in your car and you will not be in your office either. Do you want to leave your mobile phone in your car or do you want to take it with you? Briefcase mobile phones are coming on to the market, and you could put the handset in the breast pocket of your coat. You might even want to have the mobile phone in your office; cellular mobile telephone services can also be used to bypass the local telephone carrier. Although there are no cost savings at present, there might very well be other benefits, such as more rapid access that bypasses the telephone office, including your own PBX.

7. *Will You Be Using Your Mobile Phone in Areas that May Not Have Cellular Service?* Not all areas of the country will have transmission providers for some time. Even if a carrier has been chosen, it may take some time for that carrier to get into operation. Several mobile phone providers offer an arrangement that allows you to use the same phone with two transmitters, one for cellular service and one for the older Improved Mobil Telephone System (IMTS). If you arrange for IMTS service you can use your mobile phone even in less populated areas where there are no cellular services.

8. *What Happens if You Want to Use Your Phone in More than One Service Area?* This will require some additional planning in selecting your carrier. For example, Bell Atlantic Mobile Systems serve Washington, Baltimore, Philadelphia, and Pittsburgh. However, the Washington–Baltimore Cellular Telephone Company serves only the two cities in its name. If you live in Washington, D.C. and drive frequently to Philadelphia you would want to sign up with Bell Atlantic so that you can be treated as one of their regular customers rather than as a "roaming" customer with another carrier. It will be less expensive.

9. *Will You Be Purchasing Mobile Phones for Your Staff?* You may be able to negotiate quantity discounts not only on the purchase price but also on the monthly service fees.

Although there may not be service in your area now, in many instances there will be cellular service soon. If the number of automobiles on the road is any indication of the popularity of cellular mobile service, as it is in Los Angeles, Houston, Dallas, and other wide area cities, entrepreneurs will quickly take advantage of these business opportunities. You might also find that your service area is so loaded with users that you have to endure busy signals, wondering why you purchased the service. But you can expect that as demand increases the number of cells will be increased and new frequencies/channels will be allocated to already operating companies and new companies.

DON'T OVERLOOK OTHER MOBILE COMMUNICATIONS OPTIONS

Cellular mobile telephone communications has not made the other options we showed in Table 9.1 obsolete. Paging and dispatch systems can be effective if you recognize how they can serve your particular management needs and style. And for those of you who caught the CB radio bug several years ago, don't overlook its possibilities as well as its strong limitations. Simply, you should try to choose the right technology for the right job.

Radio Telephone Systems

For years mobile phone services were called mobile radio. A single radio transmitter was used to serve a radius of up to about 75 miles. The FCC set aside limited frequencies for these services, and these were quickly filled by businesses that recognized the benefits they could gain by having a telephone in their car or truck. Users shared channels or "lines" and waited long and impatiently for a dial tone. And when they got online there was often a great deal of interference and fading as they drove along the highway. Needless to say, this wasn't a very convenient way to communicate, but demand soon outstripped the supply of mobile radio services. These services are being replaced by Cellular Mobile Telephone Systems. But you can still obtain these improved mobile telephone systems as they are now called.

The procedure for acquiring radio telephone services is identical to what you need to do to acquire cellular mobile telephone services. Equipment suppliers, many of whom are now providing cellular phones, will arrange for you to use the appropriate frequencies that have been set aside for radio telephone services. As we noted in our discussion of cellular mobile services, there are some areas where cellular mobile carriers are not yet available and you may want to shift from your cellular equipment and carrier to your radio telephone transmitter and carrier.

Paging Systems

You don't have to be a physician or a plumber to use a paging system. Many firms outfit all of their senior executives with a pager to be worn on their belt or carried in their breast pocket. It's the easiest and cheapest way the chief executive can contact them when he or she really needs them. And in today's highly competitive and rapidly changing business environment you never know when you will need your chief engineer or controller. Imagine that you are at a critical point in the negotiations for that all-important loan agreement and the bank suddenly throws a curve at you. A quick call to your office discovers that your controller is "somewhere out of the office." In less than 5 minutes, with a paging system, he or she is on the line filling the important gaps in your loan applications.

Paging systems and services are emergency calling services. Managers are always facing emergencies that cost or make money. Executives want to be on the scene quickly in case of employee difficulties, or production line disruptions, or when the chairperson calls. Paging enables the manager to maintain contact and control and perhaps, more important, gives the staff the assurance that the manager is involved and as interested in the success of their activities as they are. You should consider paging technology as a low-cost potentially high-return insurance policy.

It is not difficult to acquire paging services from one of the many providers throughout the country. There are usually several in your area listed under "Paging and Signalling Equipment and Services." Purchasing paging services can be a one-stop process. Most providers are the common carriers who will not only rent you the pager but will also provide you with the transmission services, all for one monthly price. The monthly cost depends on the area you wish to cover and the extras you want on the pager. For example, a limited area coverage of unlimited call paging service with a simple "beeper" leases in the range of $17 to $25 per month for equipment, transmission, and maintenance. Should you want to purchase the equipment, it might cost you in the neighborhood of $150 to $180, and you will pay about $8 per month for unlimited calls. Wider area coverage increases the costs as do extras on the "beeper," such as a signal light that you can use instead of the tone when you are at the movies or at a concert. Additional costs will buy you an alphanumeric display of the number calling you that allows you to bypass the paging operator.

Dispatch Systems

Although paging services can be leased and you can get started with a minimum of fuss, obtaining radio dispatch services is up to you. Not only must you either obtain a license or share the required transmission channel or channels, you must provide your own dispatcher. Clearly if you are managing an operation that is providing timely services or products via trucks or automobiles throughout a large area, where the cost of late deliveries can mean many thousands of dollars (e.g., food and produce) and where unnecessary trips can waste fuel dollars, you need to be able to tightly control your fleets. In this case, operating a dispatch service may certainly be worth a major investment. However, it is becoming increasingly difficult to obtain channels. And the limited coverage and frequent interference encountered by those who do use this service are causing a shift of users to cellular mobile telephone service. Cellular mobile offers the ability to carry on conversations with your people, with no third party in between.

Citizen's Band Radio (CB Radio)

CB radio is rarely, if ever, used by executives other than for their own amusement. The citizen's band is one big party line and everyone is listening in not only for messages that might be addressed to them but for anything that is interesting. If you and some members of your executive team are already CB enthusiasts, don't overlook the use of the CB for just keeping in touch, even if for no other reason than to maintain that all-important social link executive teams need in order to be productive. In today's highly mobile world, it is not at all uncommon for members of the management team to see one another only at monthly staff meetings. Carefully worded or coded CB conversations can fill in the gaps.

WHAT'S AHEAD IN MOBILE COMMUNICATIONS?

Some airlines are offering in-flight telephone services for the traveling executive.

In the works are cellular mobile telephone services from your car to your salesperson who may be driving in a city not merely across town but across the nation. The FCC has awarded licenses to several firms who will interconnect a mobile telephone switching office in one city to a mobile telephone switching office in another city by satellite. Now that several Western European countries are also getting their plans in order for cellular mobile services it will not be long before you will be able to communicate from your automobile while driving down Fifth Avenue with your client driving down the Champs Elysees or the Ginza.

Cellular mobile telephone opens up the possibility of a telephone on every wrist (shades of Dick Tracy).

Some day it will seem absurd to ring a telephone when it is the person, not the instrument, you are trying to find. Each of us will have a personal rather than a residential telephone number and be reachable anywhere in the world.

10
FACSIMILE
TRANSMISSION

MEET "FAX"—SHORT FOR FACSIMILE TRANSMISSION

Great for Text, Drawing, and There's No Keyboarding

Mary, a civil engineer, usually takes a ribbing when she's on the road because she travels with an extra suitcase or two. She is a member of the field staff of a large foreign automobile manufacturer who is building its own chain of U.S. warehouses. Somebody is always quipping a one-liner about her traveling with enough clothes for a fashion show. The fact is, however, that one item of her luggage carries a "fax" machine—a barely 20 pound unit that can hook to any telephone and transfer a page of drawings or text back to company headquarters in less than 1 minute. This allows Mary to act on design changes in a matter of minutes rather than days.

Like its predecessor the wire-photo machine, facsimile transmission allows for the communication of images to be transmitted via wire or broadcasting. To the everyday eye, the operation of a "fax" machine is like putting materials into a photocopy machine at one end of the line and having the copy come out at the other. Like Mary says, "It's great for drawings, text, and there's no keyboarding."

A recent national survey reported that "exchanging documents" was among the top three activities in which managers engaged during their busy days. The survey also reported that managers most wanted to have the typed original page, and if not that then a high grade copy. This was a reminder that even in this age of electronic information, most managers still want to hold a printed page in their hands. It is no surprise, therefore, that facsimile transmission is such a rapidly growing business and that Mary is so pleased with her portable fax machine.

Some Background on Fax

Facsimile machines of varying types have been available since late in the nineteenth century. For most of their history, they have been used by newspapers for the transmission of wirephotos. Since the late 1960's, facsimile machines have become sufficiently reduced in price so that they have become a readily obtainable office technology.

Most facsimile machines "read" pages by rotating the material to be transmitted on a drum that is scanned by a light beam. The image (including text) is coded in terms of reflections that vary in intensity according to the tones of the original image. These variations are transduced into electrical impulses that are sent either by analog or digital processes over a communications link (usually a phone line) to a receiving machine. Some of the newest, popular facsimile machines require less than a minute per page for transmission. Of course, if you wish to implement a fax system, you have to buy or lease machines for each location on your network. You can also consider using fax services offered by third party vendors (e.g., currently the most important is Federal Express's "ZapMail"). The main distinction from their usual courier service is that your materials are sent by facsimile transmission between Federal Express offices rather than by air (see Chapter 13, Telemail).

The most immediate advantage is that facsimile machines can readily transmit graphics, any types of images, typeface design, and even photographs (with varying quality) as part of the message. This is in contrast to text-based electronic technologies that are dependent on printer capabilities for message transmission. Fax machines have been especially useful for sending text in languages (e.g., Chinese, Japanese, and Arabic) for which standard computer printing codes either are not available or are very expensive.

ACQUIRING FAX EQUIPMENT

Features of Fax Equipment

You should probably avoid leasing or buying a fax machine unless you have a major use for it. (Contracting for item-by-item fax service might be better, as you can do with the aforementioned ZapMail.) On the other hand, like Mary, you may gain substantial managerial advantages by being able to transmit text or images almost instantly between any two points on a network with compatible fax equipment. If you can see advantages in your line of work, then you will want to look into leasing or buying your own fax equipment.

Leasing or purchasing a facsimile machine is relatively expensive. Leasing can range from $200 to $800 per month, while purchasing can cost between $5,000 and $20,000. These figures do not take into account the long distance telephone costs. When you pay more for a fax machine, you are generally purchasing increased reliability, speed, as well as a variety of special automatic features. A summary of these is given in Table 10.1.

Remember that as you plan your investment you must have system compatibility with the machines at the other end of the line. In fact, a major disadvantage of facsimile transmission is the lack of equipment standardization. But you can expect this to change as equipment is more widely marketed.

Facsimile machines currently fall into three groups:

1. Systems that optically scan a page, then transmit the variations in electronic form, a process which takes 4 to 6 minutes per page.
2. Systems that employ an analog scan but use data compression techniques so as to reduce the page transmission time to 2 to 3 minutes.
3. Systems that typically use digital techniques to compress the signal for transmission and take less than one minute per page.

Tips for Making the Best of Fax

Being relatively complicated devices, fax machines require service as well as customer assistance from time to time. When you

Table 10.1. Features of Modern Facsimile Machines

Activity reporting. Keeps a record of copies sent or received, the starting and completion times, durations, and identification codes.

Auto-dial. Machine stores frequently dialed phone numbers, and will dial them either on command or as programmed by a timer.

Automatic paper feed. Enters successive copies to be transmitted into the machine automatically with no delay in transmission.

Contrast control. Has the ability to vary contrasts on demand, including automated features for matching lightness or darkness.

Encryption compatibility. Allows for communication with other digital units using scramblers or other forms of coding.

Mode matching. Before transmitting the machine matches modes with the receiving unit (by group), then selects this for fax transmission speeds.

Password Check. When the machine polls the other station for materials, passwords are checked between the two systems for compatibility.

Polling. The ability to receive documents without an operator present at the remote location; your machine interrogates and requests service from the sending machine. (This is especially advantageous for sending copies when transmission rates are low.)

Self-diagnostics. The ability of the machine to warn you of trouble and in many cases to specify the nature of it.

Step-down. Reduces the transmission rate so that copy clarity can be improved over a given network.

Voice stand-by. The capability for easily shifting between document and voice transmission over the same line (but not both at once).

purchase or lease be sure that the service is close at hand. Perhaps you can contract for it.

Are you acquiring the appropriate facsimile service for your needs? If your typical transmissions are relatively short and your use of facsimile relatively infrequent, then going to the fast and higher cost systems may not be for you. In fact, you may wish to investigate third party services.

Are supplies readily available? Many fax machines use special thermal paper, and since this varies widely in formats and standards, you want to be sure that your type is readily available.

Again, remember that fax requires machines at both ends. Even if you make a substantial investment in fax, your system will only be useful to you if the parties with whom you wish to communicate have similar capabilities.

PART THREE

NEW SERVICES AND
APPLICATIONS

11
TELEBANKING

ARE YOU ON THE ELECTRONIC MONEY NETWORK?

From the *Los Angeles Times*, Tuesday, June 11, 1985:

> The Supreme Court cleared the way Monday for what could become a broad reshaping of the nation's banking system, ruling that states may create regional banking zones to protect their own institutions from big, expansion-minded banks with headquarters outside the area . . . . More recently, big bank holding companies have moved across state lines offering "non-bank" services such as credit cards . . . .
>
> Faced with growing competition from such operations, some states began following an alternative course, allowing the merger and expansion of local and regional banks without permitting unimpeded interstate banking from all over the country . . . . This is the last great industry in the U.S. to consolidate.
>
> We don't know today the names of the 10 most powerful banks of 1985 because they're still in the formative stage . . . .

When the merchants in the Middle Ages ceased carrying their wealth on their backs and the new bankers accepted the merchant's name as credit, banking became an information business. Information is money. Information transmitted on telecommunications networks is electronic money. And the faster you can move your money, the more money you make. Regional banking, national banking, credit, debit, "smart" cards, automatic teller and point of sale machines—all of these represent a revolution in banking that has taken place with the telecommunications revolution. If banking is changing so radically, shouldn't your banking habits and practices also change?

The following is how you can benefit by being on the electronic money networks, or by *telebanking:*

> You have tighter control over your money.
>
> Telebanking reduces the float of incoming monies.
>
> You gain discounts and other benefits that can reduce your cash outlays and you do not have to lose your float.
>
> There are new services that track your receivables around the world, allowing you to better plan tomorrow's financial transactions.
>
> Telebanking products and services give you an accurate picture of your real cash balance 24 hours per day.
>
> Online services deliver real time stock and futures quotes from worldwide markets and allow you to trade around-the-clock, around-the-world.
>
> Telebanking products and services enable you to analyze your investment portfolios continuously for tax planning and investment opportunities.
>
> New, widely available services provide you with information about money, about interest rates and their trends, about the money markets, and about the national and the world economy, information you need to know in order to do financial planning.

THE IMPORTANCE OF CHOOSING THE RIGHT FINANCIAL SERVICES FIRM

Telebanking with Banks

Not all banks offer telebanking services. The high cost of telecommunications networks and switches has made it difficult for many banks to provide telebanking unless they can share telecommunications facilities with other banks. However, this has not always been possible. The comptroller of the currency and state bank regulators have been most conscientious in maintaining a highly competitive dual banking system and have believed that sharing telecommunications networks could result in less competition. However, the economics of networks are different from the economics of local banking. You need a larger geographic area with more potential customers than is usually assigned to the local bank, for electronic banking to be economical.

Banking has joined the consolidation trend and bank borders are vanishing. Some states now permit entry, under certain conditions, of banks from any other state and some states permit interstate banking on a regional basis. Other states have yet to make their decision. National or regional banking will stimulate telebanking. To take advantage of the benefits you can gain from telebanking, you might look first for a bank that serves the region in which you do your business and is likely to expand its telebanking facilities and services. Table 11.1 summarizes regional and national banking states.

Table 11.1. Regional and National Banking States

States That Permit Banks from Any State to do Business		
Arizona		
Maine		
New York		
Rhode Island		
South Dakota		
Regional Banking Arrangements		
New England		
Connecticut		
Massachusetts		
Southeast		
Florida	North Carolina	Virginia
Georgia	South Carolina	
Maryland	Tennessee	
Midcentral		
Indiana		
Kentucky		
West		
Idaho	Utah	
Nevada	Washington	
Oregon		

Telebanking with the Nonbanks

Just as competition in telecommunications offers you a number of options heretofore unavailable to you, so does competition in banking offer a host of new options for your banking. There are the so-called nonbanks, such as the financial services offered by American Express, Sears, Merrill Lynch, Bank One, and merchandising and brokerage firms that have recognized that money and telebanking offers them opportunities to provide financial services that are essentially competitive to the traditional banks.

Although many of these operations are geared to the consumer rather than business services, they do offer packages that are attractive for the business executive. And what's more, they are pioneers in the innovative uses of telecommunications for the delivery of financial and information services. You are likely to find them employing the telephone, cable television, videotex terminals, personal computers, and the smaller inexpensive home computers as a basis for offering their telebanking products and services.

These nonbanks, however, are not merchant bankers who can provide you with loans or factor your accounts. But they can provide services to assist you in tax and investment planning. It is important to you that they are nationwide services if you and your staff provide services across the country.

Telebanking on Consumer Information Services

The personal computer spurred the development of a number of network information services firms, such as The Source and CompuServe. These firms are unique in that they are not equipment suppliers, nor do they own the networks on which they operate or the information they often provide. They are information providers, in a way information middlemen or brokers who sell access to databases, information, and programs that assist you in making decisions with this data and information. These services are currently experimenting with telebanking where essentially they provide the link between you and the bank. Because these services are changing rapidly, your best method for obtaining information will be to call or write the service directly; names and addresses are given in Chapter 12.

Financial Information Services

Consumer information services, especially Dow Jones News/Retrieval, offer a wide variety of financial information databases, including current market news, current quotes, historical quotes, historical averages, and (via Dow Jones) access to Disclosure II (SEC information), Media General Financial Services, the *Weekly Economic Survey*, and the *Forbes Directory*. Also newly available are special software packages for accessing these services, "downloading" information from them, and for performing your own custom tailored analyses. (Information on software can be obtained from your local computer dealer or, for the Dow Jones line, from the address given in Chapter 12.)

ACQUIRING YOUR TELEBANKING SERVICES

From a Bank or Financial Services Provider

Find out whether telebanking options are offered where you are doing your banking now. Your current financial services provider (bank or nonbank) may be able to provide you with the equipment necessary to use the online services. This is usually the best alternative because you will still be doing business with a bank you know; only the means for transactions are being expanded. Or if your current banking service is not moving into telebanking, perhaps another nearby institution is.

Any institution offering telebanking services should be able to recommend the equipment you need and assist you in purchasing or leasing it. In many cases the equipment required to access the service can be used for other purposes, such as telemail or word processing. Consequently, you may wish to purchase the equipment rather than lease it. Mostly, the current alternatives for transaction services are a computer terminal (or personal computer) and telephone network combination.

From a Network Information Service

Again, these vendors are intermediaries, but they may be able to connect you with financial transactions or information services. For a start, you can contact The Source or CompuServe (see Chapter 12) to see what is available, or local banks or financial institutions for suggestions. It is likely, too, that specialized services will be available in the near future. For example, several banks have joined forces with AT&T to offer nationwide electronic information services aimed at small business and the consumer. A network of banks and brokerage houses throughout the nation will be linked to provide financial information and transactional services that can be accessed by personal computers and other terminals that will be offered by AT&T and other firms. It is likely that small, special purpose terminals will be offered, capable of performing simple banking transactions that will be made available at low cost to users who do not wish to purchase more general use computer terminals or personal computers.

There are also new "receive only" financial information services. Some are becoming available via cable television services, from public television stations, or from specialized carrier services available over FM radio. (The latter operates with a pocket-size portable receiver.) Again, these are one-way services designed to provide immediate stock and futures quotes. You can then use your telephone to perform your transactions.

12
TELERESEARCHING
(Databases)

I was sitting in a hotel in Chicago when it dawned on me that I ought to fit another major bank into my sales calls for the day. After using my lap computer to dial into Dow Jones News/Retrieval, I found the names of the corporate officers, the balance sheet for last year, and insights into the bank's specialties in the Chicago money market. This was my first step in turning a potentially "cold" contact into a warm prospect . . . .

CAROLE E. (VIDEO EQUIPMENT SALES)

TAKING ADVANTAGE OF NETWORK INFORMATION SERVICES

Going "Online" for Your Information Needs

Hardly less than a decade ago, if you needed specialized information (e.g., a government research report, a financial profile of a major corporation, or references to psychological research on age and task performance), you had to go digging for it. This typically meant extra time spent in a research library or waiting weeks for the answers to be mailed to you from some remote source. Or it meant the valuable time of your staff being wasted in sometimes endless legwork. Today, much of this information is available to you right on the screen of your personal computer if you take advantage of the new "network information services." You use your computer to communicate over telephone lines to an "information provider," who, usually for an initial subscription fee, an hourly connect charge, and sometimes a publisher's royalty, can deliver about any type of information that has been stored in a database. (The subscription provides you with identification and password codes, plus telephone numbers for low-cost long distance access as we described in Chapter 7.) Some of these new services are both increasingly available and inexpensive.

The Worlds of Information Utilities and Databases

The growth of network information services has been so brisk that it is difficult to keep track of the offerings or even to classify them. There are distinctions among "videotext" (sometimes "videotex"), "database," and "teletext" services. Videotext, a service that is offered over telephone or cable television systems, allows you to access information on "pages" much as you read a newspaper or search through a telephone directory. There is limited interactive capability for enabling you to search a library for specific words, phrases, or documents. Databases range all the way from electronic information files from which you can retrieve data to user-oriented information services either in themselves or as a part of a videotext service. The better database services offer many options for rapid searching and retrieval—for example, you could search through newspaper files looking for a designated key word or phrase.

Teletext is typically associated with the broadcast medium in that it comprises pages of information (and sometimes graphics) that are "piggybacked" on a television signal. Your special receiver stores current "pages" that you can retrieve by use of a keyboard or pad. It is less interactive than videotext or database uses because the information file is restricted to what has been "captured" in the local unit. Teletext systems have typically been home-consumer oriented services marketed by newspaper and broadcasting companies and are not of interest to us here.

Mostly, the services of use to a business person are of the videotext and database nature and fall into four general categories:

Information Utilities: These are companies that provide a wide range of databases, somewhat akin to an "electronic publisher" or "gateway" service to use terms from the trade. Often mail and shopping services ("online" services following) are included among the options.

Information Retrieval Services: Some companies specialize in certain types of database information—for example, engineering data. They may be gateway systems to a set of databases.

Specific Databases: Many databases are available for direct use.

Online Services: There is a growing number of companies that offer specialized services, such as travel schedules or shopping; these are more a transactional service than a database as such.

INFORMATION UTILITIES

Inexpensive Publicly Available Services

The so-called information utilities are those companies that make a wide variety of low-cost services available, especially those of interest to the public (financial information, news, references, and sometimes bulletin boards, "electronic mail," or games). They also often serve as "gateways" to shopping services, travel information, or specialized databases. Information utilities are marketed in hopes of attracting a large public audience. Although their prices do vary, all require an initial subscription fee (e.g., The Source is $50), all offer very low nighttime rates (around $6 per hour at 300 baud, the speed of transmission), and if there is a monthly minimum, it is usually not over $10. Within the last several years, there have been many special price opportunities, such as getting a free subscription when you purchase a modem. We will describe four main companies in this business: Dow Jones News/Retrieval, The Source, CompuServe, and Delphi.

Dow Jones News/Retrieval

Dow Jones & Company, Inc.
P.O. Box 300
Princeton, NJ 08540
(800/257-5114)
(in New Jersey 609/452-1511)

As you can readily guess, Dow Jones News/Retrieval is operated by the publishers of the *Wall Street Journal* and *Barron's*, the long-time providers of market information. Although its main offerings are business information, including files from its publications, the service has been adding other items of interest. For example, you can send MCI mail, check general news headlines, consult the *Official Airline Guides Electronic Edition*, use Comp-U-Store, access the *Academic American Encyclopedia*, and get sports news or even movie reviews. One of the most powerful features offered by Dow Jones News/Retrieval is their "text search." By using any combination of words, dates, or numbers, you can search through the Dow Jones files for anything published since June 1979. In addition to regular rates, you pay special fees for uses of certain databases. This service offers the most for the business person.

The Source

Source Telecomputing Corporation
1616 Anderson Road
McLean, VA 22102
(703/734-7500; 800/336-3366)

The Source is a subsidiary of The Reader's Digest Association, Inc. When you subscribe to The Source, you receive a well edited and organized handbook. Its contents are divided into sections describing services for communications, news, business, consumer information, entertainment, publishing, travel, education, and computing services. One of the valuable features of The Source is access to the recent UPI newswire files. Using a relatively simple command system, you can literally search the world's news for any specific topic. The Source's mail and bulletin board systems seem to enjoy wide use. (You may notice that some people are now listing their Source ID along with their mailing addresses.) It is very easy to initiate a letter to send via The Source, either one you type directly online or "upload" from your disk files. The Source can offer you mail service to a number of countries outside the United States.

CompuServe

Consumer Information Service
5000 Arlington Centre Boulevard
P.O. Box 20212
Columbus, OH 43220
(800/848-8990)

CompuServe has many of the same major features as The Source, including, for example, mail, conferencing, bulletin boards, direct communications, news, business items, programs, programming, educational information, and shopping. However, CompuServe offers a much greater selection of interest group or bulletin board types of alternatives, particularly on topics of a hobbyist nature. If your needs are in business information, you can subscribe to CompuServe's "Executive Information Service" along with their regular service. CompuServe's monthly magazine, *Online Today*, is particularly useful.

Delphi

General Videotex Corporation
3 Blackstone Street
Cambridge, MA 02139
(617/491-3393)

Delphi is a smaller online information service than those just described; however, it is very well designed, and so easy to use that you notice this unique quality. It has an efficient encyclopedia service and offers access to other services, such as Dialog. Delphi has been experimenting with a unique service whereby you can initiate mail that can be sent to members of other information utilities. One of the special premiums of Delphi is that you can obtain 1200 baud service for the same price as 300 baud.

INFORMATION RETRIEVAL SERVICES

Online Libraries

These are the modern version of the databases that reference libraries used to access on our behalf in past years. They are designed for specialized users (scientists, researchers, business persons, physicians) and are sometimes much more expensive to use than information utilities. Also, some may require training in order to maximize their use.

Dialog

Dialog Information Services
Marketing Dept.
3460 Hillview Avenue
Palo Alto, CA 94304
(800/227-1927)
(in California 800/982-5838)

Among the best known of the professional oriented database services is Dialog Information Services, Inc. It is considerably more expensive than the previously mentioned "utilities" (or BRS/After Dark below); a 10 minute search might run $10 to $15, but there are no start-up or subscription fees. (When inquiring, ask about their "Knowledge Index" service, a reduced price option.) Dialog's nearly 200 databases cover science, technology, chemistry, medicine, engineering, social sciences, business, economics, and current events. Dialog also offers regular training sessions for new users.

Nexis

Marketing Department
Mead Data Central
P.O. Box 1830
Dayton, OH 45401
(800/227-4908)

Nexis is the premier among services that offer retrieval from major periodicals, including the wire services and *The New York Times*. You can retrieve entire texts using a variety of search procedures including key words. Like the other professionally oriented services, Nexis is expensive. There is an initial fee for a terminal, a monthly subscription fee, plus hourly and surcharge costs, depending on how you use the service. Nexis also offers Lexis, an online retrieval service for legal information.

NewsNet

NewsNet
945 Haverford Road
Bryn Mawr, PA 19010
(800/345-1301)
(in Pennsylvania 215/527-8030)

Just about every specialized area of business is served by a professional newsletter, sometimes many of them. These newsletters are often very expensive and are not easily found in traditional libraries. NewsNet is a service that currently offers access to nearly 200 business newsletters, in addition to United Press International and a special public relations newswire. You pay an hourly rate (currently $15) for NewsNet, plus special surcharges that vary by newsletter.

Tech Data

Information Handling Services
15 Inverness Way East
Englewood, CO 80150
(303/790-0600)

Tech Data is an engineering oriented database service that includes industrial catalogs, standards, military and federal specifications, bibliographies, and other technologically oriented files. Registration is $50 per year, connect charges are $100 per hour with a monthly $15 minimum.

Instant Yellow Page Service

Instant Yellow Page Service
5707 S. 86th Circle
P.O. Box 27347
Omaha, NE 68127
(402/331-7169)

You can access any of the over 4800 Yellow Page telephone directories in this country from Instant Yellow Page Service, which is online 24 hours a day. You can gather data by region as well as business type and even print address labels.

BRS/After Dark

BRS/After Dark
1200 Rt. 7
Latham, NY 12100
(800/833-4707)
(800/553-5566 in New York state)
(518/783-7251 from Alaska, Hawaii and outside the United States)

The initials stand for Bibliographic Retrieval Service, and the After Dark refers to the fact that it offers low cost access to bibliographies during non-prime-time hours, namely nights and weekends. BRS/After Dark offers an easily used system for online access to approximately 80 databases including the sciences, medicine, business and finance, reference, education, social sciences, and humanities. Charges are according to level of usage, the least being a $55 yearly password fee, a basic connect rate of $35 per hour ($10 month minimum), plus a small royalty to database vendors.

SPECIFIC DATABASES

If you have highly specialized needs, you may wish to inquire if there is a specific database to satisfy them. Often such specialized databases can be accessed directly, although the procedures might be a bit more complex than the more popular services. Major guides to specialized databases include:

Databasics. New York: Garland Publishing Co.

Database Directory. White Plains, NY: Knowledge Industry Publications, Inc.

Directory of Online Databases. Los Angeles: Cuadra Associates.

The Executive's Guide to Online Information Services. White Plains, NY: Knowledge Industry Publications, Inc.

CONSUMER ONLINE SERVICES

A Growing Business

In the last several years, there has been a steady growth in services directed to popular consumer needs—for example, shopping, travel schedules, encyclopedias, or banking. As previously mentioned, these are often available via an information utility. (The utility links you with the service company's computer.) The following are two popular examples of such services.

Official Airlines Guides—Electronic Edition

Official Airline Guides—Electronic Edition
200 Clearwater Drive
Oak Brook, IL 60521
(312/654-6000; 800/323-4000)
(800/942-3011 in Illinois)

In a nutshell, the online *Guide* will give you the latest information on airline schedules and fares. You cannot book a reservation via this service, although this capability is likely to be possible in the near future. Like its printed counterpart, the *Official Airline Guide* is invaluable for trip planning. It not only saves you time with your travel agent, but will show you alternatives that either your agent might overlook or a competing airline might not be inclined to find for you. The *Guide* requires a one-time subscription of $50 and a usage charge, but no monthly minimum.

Comp-U-Store

Compu-U-Card International, Inc.
777 Summer Street
Stamford, CT 06901
(203/324-9261)

Comp-U-Store is a shopping service that has some 50,000 items listed in its electronic catalog. These are goods ranging from television and audio equipment to the best sterling tableware, all of which they claim to offer at discount prices. You typically access Comp-U-Store via an information utility; however, it is necessary to buy a membership (currently $25). You do this either through the host services or by contacting the company directly.

A FEW TIPS

Before you subscribe to expensive professional services, be sure that you need them. Remember that most major libraries can assist you with research, or if you have a special task, call on a consultant.

If you are watching your telecommunications budget, be cautious about subscribing to services with a monthly minimum, especially if automatically paid by a charge card. Even $10 or $15 adds up across a few months, especially if you are not using the service extensively.

For more costly services, study the user's manual for the least time-consuming methods for getting what you want.

If you are using a personal computer, remember that it might be handy to copy your transactions onto a disk file so you can have information in computer-readable form. (There are methods for moving data into your own spreadsheets or database programs.)

Inquire about the availability of special software for using a service. Often this greatly simplifies the use as well as saving on connect charges.

13

TELEMAILING

NO MORE TRIPS TO THE POST OFFICE

Karl's discovery of the convenience of creating and mailing letters from his personal computer keyboard is typical of the stories you hear about the new electronic mail services. As a project developer on the staff of a large construction company, Karl often got the jump on his competition by submitting his preliminary bid proposals by Western Union Mailgrams™ that he would dictate over the telephone. When it became possible to originate them from his personal computer, this was especially attractive because Karl could keep certain key paragraphs stored on word processing discs, then adapt them for different projects. Karl is not only ahead of his competition, but he can skip those pesky trips to the post office, rummaging around for stamps, or bothering with stationery and envelopes. Moreover, Karl can create and dispatch mail while he is on the road. All he needs is his portable terminal and a telephone line.

Karl's story is a new chapter in a service that computer buffs have gloated over for years—the ability to send messages to one another instantaneously, not having to depend on the post office and being able to avoid frustrating ''telephone tag.'' Mostly such ''telemail,'' as we call it, was restricted to individuals in large computer networks in the military, major corporations, or universities. Now virtually anybody with access to a computer or word processor can

Table 13.1. The Major Mail Services

Computer-Based Mail Services

MCI Mail
2000 M Street, NW
Washington, DC, 20036
(202/293-4255).

EasyLink Instant Mail
P.O. Box 37472
Omaha, NE 68137
(800/445-4444)

Facsimile Delivery Service

ZapMail Service
Federal Express
(dial your local office as
listed in the phone directory)

Information Utilities Offering Electronic Mail

Source Telecomputing Corporation
1616 Anderson Road
McLean, VA 22102
(703/734-7500; 800/336-3366)

Delphi
General Videotex Corporation
3 Blackstone Street
Cambridge, MA 02139
(617/491-3393)

Consumer Information Service
5000 Arlington Centre Boulevard
P. O. Box 20212
Columbus, OH 43220
(800/848-8990)

send mail over the telephone network. Or if you are not inclined to use computer-based mail services, there is ''ZapMail,'' where your letter, document, or blueprints are sent as facsimile images between Federal Express offices to be hand delivered within two hours from origination.

All of these services are part of the growing business of ''electronic mail'' where competitors ranging from Federal Express to Western Union are vying for your business. Table 13.1 contains a summary of the major services and their addresses.

A GLIMPSE AT MAJOR COMPUTER-BASED SERVICES

Service at Your Fingertips

The new world of electronic mail presents you with a range of alternatives varying in price, convenience, and speed. All of the computer-based services are currently restricted to sending text or data. Graphics can be sent only if they are constructed from regular alphanumeric characters. (For sending graphics materials, see Facsimile Transmission in Chapter 10 and ZapMail on page 140.)

Computer-to-Computer

The most fundamental form of electronic mail involves an end-to-end (total) computer linkage from sender to receiver. Essentially you originate a letter on your computer or word processor, dispatch it to a mail service via the telephone network where it is stored in a central computer. When your addressee logs into the mail service, a note indicates awaiting mail. It can then be read or ''downloaded'' into your addressee's computer for storage or printing. In the case of correspondence other than brief notes, you will usually want to prepare and edit the letter ''offline'' with your word processor or word processing program, then ''upload'' it on linking into the mail service. For short memos, most of the services have editing capabilities so you can create a message directly ''online,'' which is handy if you are on the road with your lap computer.

A critical requirement for computer-to-computer mail is that your addressee either regularly or by agreement with you checks for incoming mail. Otherwise the awaiting letter will sit unread in the central file. As mentioned subsequently, many mail services give you the option of having the letter printed, then mailed or delivered, but the cost is greater and the speed slower than direct computer transmittal.

Computer-to-computer mail is efficient if you are in regular contact with an addressee, or if there are advantages to exchanging text in computer-readable form. For example, an insurance investigator described to us how he regularly filed electronic reports via his portable computer while on fact-finding trips. His secretary back in Chicago would download the draft reports, then assemble them (without retyping) in a weekly summary for the company. You might consider a similar application while writing during trips. Send the files to yourself, then when back home either load them into your personal computer for further editing, or have them processed directly at your office. Also, it is now possible with a little ingenuity to send data files by regular electronic mail services, then ''read'' the information into database or spreadsheet programs.

Three of the major information utilities (CompuServe, The Source, Delphi) offer direct mail service, as do MCI Mail and EasyLink, who also offer alternative delivery options. Increasingly most of these services either offer or recommend software packages that allow you to automate dialing, log on steps, and facilitate use of the usual mail-handling functions.

Computer-to-Surface Mail

MCI Mail and Western Union's EasyLink service give you the option of having your computer-originated mail printed at a service office nearest your addressee then forwarded via the U.S. Postal Service. (The Postal Service has discontinued its own ''ECOM'' which was never aggressively marketed.)

MCI print format is professionally attractive and your letter arrives in an 8-by-11-inch eye-catching orange envelope. For an extra fee, you can have your letterhead as well as facsimile signature regularly appear on the printed letter. EasyLink's postal format is their familiar Mailgram™ service. Both services have options for sending overseas mail.

The advantage of computer-to-surface mail, of course, is that your addressee need not be a member of the mail network, use a computer, or be checking into a service. The other is that your letter arrives in a neatly printed format. Both services also make it very easy to send the same letter to multiple addresses or a distribution list. Finally, there is the convenience factor; you can originate a neatly printed letter from virtually anywhere you can get your computer linked into the telephone network.

We've encountered some true innovators on this latter point. One colleague of ours in chemical sales regularly carries his lap computer while making calls. He follows up each meeting with a brief thank-you letter (written in a hotel room or on the airplane) that summarizes the order. A printed copy is dispatched to his client and an electronic ''carbon copy'' is picked up by the home office to place the order.

The only serious discouraging note we've encountered with these services is that unless you keep track of the file numbers of your messages, it is difficult to follow up on an undelivered letter. In fact it might take weeks before an undelivered letter finds its way back to you. One tip, then, is to request your addressee to acknowledge receipt. A more minor note is that we've heard of several instances where the brightly colored MCI envelope was mistaken as advertising and went unopened.

Computer-to-Other Services

Both MCI and EasyLink offer access to Telex delivery. Western Union's EasyLink further connects with their overnight Mailgram™ service, telegrams (delivered within hours), as well as overseas cablegrams.

Computer-to-Courier

Courier rather than postal service delivery is available from MCI Mail and EasyLink for an additional fee. In both cases, you have your choice of a 24 hour or an immediate service, with a major price difference, of course. The rapid service is currently restricted to major cities in the United States, but there are alternatives for international delivery.

For mail to major U.S. cities during the day, you could originate a letter on your computer keyboard, dispatch it to one of these services, and anticipate that it will be in the hands of your addressee within four hours.

A courier service is excellent for last minute items, such as proposals, bids, or documents where printed copy is critical and a telephone call is insufficient. It has its innovative uses too. We know of one contractor who rewrote his presentation early one morning on his portable computer in a hotel room and had the printed copy delivered to himself at the afternoon meeting where it was duplicated and distributed.

IS IT DIFFICULT TO USE?

Is the "computer" aspect of electronic mail difficult to use? Really not. Figure 13.1 is an MCI example of logging on, checking the "Input" box, and sending a letter. The comments in brackets have been added by us.

After you dispatch your MCI letter, you are again given the master menu which allows you to create more letters, check your "in" or "out" boxes, or exit the service. MCI deserves recognition for a service that almost teaches itself to you.

Figure 13.1. An example of MCI mail

[dialed local MCI Mail number]

Port: 6.

Please enter your user name: FWILLIAMS
Password: [entered but does not show on screen]
Connection initiated. . . Opened.

Welcome to MCI Mail!

[. . . etc. some notices were included here]
MCI Mail Version 2.0

Your INBOX has 3 messages

Press ⟨RETURN⟩ to continue

You may enter: [your master menu]

SCAN	for a summary of your mail
READ	to READ messages one by one
PRINT	to display messages nonstop
CREATE	to write an MCI Letter
DOWJONES	for Dow Jones News/Retrieval
ACCOUNT	to adjust terminal display
HELP	for assistance

Command (or MENU or EXIT): SCAN [you check the mail]

You may enter:

INBOX	to SCAN your unread messages
OUTBOX	to SCAN messages you sent
DESK	to SCAN messages read before
DRAFT	to SCAN your DRAFT message
ALL	to SCAN ALL your messages
HELP	for assistance

Command (or MENU or EXIT): INBOX [check the inbox]
   3 messages in INBOX [length is omitted from the below list]

No.	Posted	From	Subject
1	Oct 21 21:00	Francis Cramp	Technology Update
2	Oct 21 21:18	Betty White	Speaker for Seminar
3	Oct 22 09:47	Herbert Dordick	Texas Presentation

Press ⟨RETURN⟩ to continue

138

Figure 13.1. (*Continued*)

You may enter:

READ   to READ the scanned messages
PRINT   to display messages nonstop
SCAN   to SCAN for other messages
HELP   for assistance

Command (or MENU or EXIT): MENU [get ready to create a letter]

[you ask for the master menu and select "CREATE"]

TO: Dr. Francis Cramp

(Dr. Francis Cramp not found. Enter a postal address or
 TLX: (telex address), type HELP, or press RETURN to delete.)

[you enter a postal mailing address]

            Annenberg School of Communications
            University of Southern California
            Los Angeles CA 90007

Subject: [you put in a subject description]

            MCI Example

CC: [If no copies to other people then press Return]

Text: (Type/on a line by itself to end)

Hi Frank:

Here is the example of MCI Mail you wanted.
Neat, isn't it?
But we can't keep meeting this way.

Best,

Fred

/   [the slash plus Return signals the end of the letter]

Press ⟨RETURN⟩ to continue [done]

[you are then given the options for sending your letter or you can request an
editing mode to make changes]

FACSIMILE-COURIER SERVICE

Not to be left behind is a new mail service offered by Federal Express: "ZapMail," a facsimile-based service. In essence, Federal Express still picks up your document but instead of delivering it by airplane, they transmit it by facsimile between their offices. A courier at the receiver's end then delivers the transmitted copy.

Federal Express sees two advantages in this service, although it is more expensive than computer-originated ones. First, the users are not dependent on computer systems. A phone call and delivery pick-up gets the process started. Second, the document is not restricted to the standard alphanumeric characters; or put more practically, you can send graphics, including blueprints.

Remember, however, that if you could benefit from frequent use of facsimile services to a given destination, consider installing your own equipment (see Chapter 10).

LOOK FOR STILL MORE INNOVATIONS

Given the convenience and decreasing expense of various forms of electronic mail, the alternatives are bound to expand, both in service options and additional vendors. At least one large urban bank has considered offering its "online" customers access to electronic mail services not only to its offices but to its other clients. You can set up a company-based telemailing system yourself in the form of a computer bulletin board (Chapter 5) for less than $5000, including the cost of the computer.

Also, the technology is in place that makes it possible for you to read your telemailed mail without a computer terminal. AT&T is rumored to be introducing a service that enables you to check your electronic mail by a telephone call; for a small fee, you can hear your mail in the form of computer generated speech.

14

TELECONFERENCING

THE MEETING THAT ALMOST DIDN'T HAPPEN

Ralph had his secretary send the urgent message to his senior staff the very morning he heard the merger talk. He wanted to meet his staff before they began to hear rumors on the street, rumors that more often than not turned out to be incorrect gossip. The meeting was to be the very next morning. Memos went out immediately and telephone calls made to the field offices. Ralph's vice president of finance could not attend; he had finally managed to snare the firm's loan committee for his presentation that very morning. The personnel manager was recovering from emergency surgery and would not be back into the office for at least another 10 days. And the field sales managers, now out of both coasts, certainly could not be at the headquarters office the next morning. This could have been a meeting that never happened.

No problem for Ralph; he had prepared for such an emergency several months before when he added a teleconferencing facility in a meeting room at the same time that he installed the new intelligent telephone system and PBX. The meeting went off as planned; the vice president of finance called into the conference from home just before he left for the bank and the personnel manager dialed the conference from his hospital bed. All went well—even better than the usual staff meeting. Everyone asked questions, even some of the junior members of Ralph's staff who otherwise might have been overwhelmed by the senior staff. Ralph controlled the meeting with his new telephone which told him who among the conferees, at home, in the hospital, or in some distant city wanted to talk, and he gave everyone a chance.

This is just one example of how teleconferencing can work for you; it can guarantee that your important meetings, indeed, all of your meetings, will be well attended.

BUYING MEETING INSURANCE WITH TELECONFERENCING

How Teleconferencing Can Work for You

As with Ralph's example, we've now had enough experiences with teleconferencing to know that it works. Here are some especially valuable benefits:

Teleconferencing can be a substitute for travel or reduce travel costs and nonproductive travel time.

Teleconferencing can ensure that the right people are always at your meetings and that your meetings will always come off as you want them to.

Teleconferencing can make meetings shorter, more efficient, and often more manageable.

Teleconferencing can make meetings more convenient by bringing the meeting to the participants rather than the participants to the meeting.

Teleconferencing can increase your span of control; keep you on top of events no matter where they may be occurring.

Teleconferencing can give you an important tactical advantage for those meetings where you must be in control.

Teleconferencing adds to your management skills by offering additional communications options for coordinating activities at remote sites as well as in your office.

Teleconferencing decreases your information gap; the time between asking for information and receiving that information can be shortened.

Teleconferencing ensures continuity in your operations when bad weather stalls your travel plans or strikes and fuel shortages make it difficult or very expensive to travel.

Teleconferencing offers another way to maintain and improve personnel relations by increasing the employee's sense of participation.

Teleconferencing increases your productivity by reducing travel fatigue.

How Teleconferencing Can Work Against You

But teleconferencing isn't all good news. Here are some cautions:

Beware of more meetings because teleconferencing is so "easy."

Teleconferencing can lower personnel morale because of decreased face-to-face contact or loss of travel perks.

Do not expect teleconferencing to replace all travel.

Teleconferencing is a new mode of working and requires planning; an unplanned teleconference can be disastrous.

Teleconferencing is an awkward way for people to meet for the first time.

Teleconferencing can control too much and be seen as "big brother."

Teleconferencing ought not to be used for tough bargaining and negotiation sessions, unless you have mastered the art of the teleconference.

Because of the lack of microphone or on-camera skills, some otherwise effective individuals do not "show up" well in teleconferences ("Hollywood effect").

As with much of new information technology, teleconferencing alters the social organization of your office and firm and could create strains on internal politics.

OPTIONS FOR TELECONFERENCING

The new telecommunications have opened a variety of tested teleconferencing options. No longer are you limited to a party line for

Table 14.1. Teleconferencing at a Glance

What It Does	Advantages	Disadvantages
Audio		
Multiparty line for voice communications. From three to as many parties as you wish for a meeting.	Easy to arrange; low cost reduces inefficient meetings because key staff can be present. Uses POTS. Works for short meetings. Good for giving orders, crises decision making, briefings, information seeking and gathering, interviewing; encourages participation.	No visual support; inability to see nonverbal clues. Lack of meeting control; poor for first impressions.
Enhanced Audio		
Audio and fax, text processing, electronic mail, computer conferencing, telewriting, data transmission, electronic blackboard, remote slide control, and U.S. Mail.	Relatively low cost and easily arranged. Can be assembled from stand-alone systems. Provides necessary visuals for efficient decision making, Provides "remote signoff" and management oversight; a multimedia environment.	Limited to still pictures and relatively low speed data and graphics transmission; relatively narrow bandwidth. Meeting coordination complex.
Video—Full Motion		
May be one-way video and two-way audio, or two-way audio and video. Wide bandwidth suitable for high speed	Simulates face-to-face meetings, suitable for complex meetings with many visuals. Good for corporate events,	High cost for two-way video can be offset by one-way video and two-way audio. Point-to-point limits partici-

data, fax, and other enhancements. High resolution for large screen projection.	demos, persuasive meetings, presentations. High degree of social presence.	pants to two locations. Requires video "production" values and must be "produced," often with scripts and directors.
Uses POTS and transmits still pictures at about one frame or picture every 30 seconds. Usually one-way video only. Additional low speed enhancements can be added as in audio-only conferences.	*Video—Slow Speed* Low cost transmission of visuals when real time video is required. Good for charts, graphs and still visual displays. Advantages of video but lacks full motion. Uses POTS.	Low cost video conferencing with disadvantages noted for video conferencing.
Interactive computer-to-computer communications; may be real time or store and forward. Can include text processing, electronic messaging and bulletin boards.	*Computer Conferencing* Provides for in-depth conferencing. Continuous discussions possible. Store and forward allows for timed responses. Allows many users; can be kept confidential. Closed conferences are possible. Allows for online record of conference.	Requires computer terminals with modems and special POTS for high speed communications. Host computer required for many participants and for storage of conversations. Small conferences without storage can use bulletin board program in PC. Comments can be permanently recorded.

your multiparty conference. No longer must you arrange the conference days in advance with remote phone operators. Further, you can enhance the audio meeting with pictures, data, or text that can be delivered while you are at your meeting. If you are the kind of an executive who thrives on personal contact, you can get pretty close to it with video conferences. Table 14.1 provides a quick glance at the teleconferencing options available to you today.

SIX STEPS TO SUCCESSFUL TELECONFERENCING

Teleconferencing is not merely an extension of your telephone; it is an important tool of your information systems. Teleconferencing adds to your executive skills by allowing you to operate across space and time by transporting your voice, image, and writings wherever there are telecommunications facilities. Teleconferencing is a management support system that enables you to increase your management skills.

Do not think about teleconferencing as simply another mix of new telecommunications technologies now being "hyped" in the many magazines you read. Think about teleconferencing as enabling you to manage in ways you could not before, for achieving your management objectives, and performing your management tasks in ways not heretofore available.

You must be serious about teleconferencing if you are going to get the most out of it. It's no longer a toy, it's not experimental, and there are many success stories you can look into. Here are six steps for successful teleconferencing.

Step One: Know What you Need

Making any information or telecommunications technology work for you is to define what it is you want to do. In the beginning of this chapter we saw Ralph rapidly set up a teleconference for his emergency staff meeting. This is just one example of what might be called ad hoc teleconferencing. Consider this second example.

A major Hollywood studio wanted to release a new film simultaneously in 27 cities. Clearly, the studio could not follow its usual promotional procedures, namely a well publicized press conference in the city that would draw the largest number of reporters, and hope that the word would spread to the other 26 cities. So the studio de-

cided to have a teleconference with three of the film's stars in Holly-
wood and reporters in the 27 cities in hotel rooms in their own cities.
The reporters saw the stars via video on a large screen and asked their
questions via a speaker phone arrangement in the room. The stars
responded much as they did in face-to-face interviews even if they
could not see their interviewers.

This conference, the first of its kind for a film studio, went especially well. More questions were asked than usual and many formerly quiet reporters, who were usually shouted down when in
one room with their more aggressive colleagues, were heard from.

Unlike Ralph's teleconference, which was relatively low cost, requiring only the telephone system, the studio conference was more
elaborate. It included one-way video with high quality large screen
projection. After all, the objective of the teleconference was for the
stars to sell their as yet unseen film, and this required an environment that capitalized on the stars' images and their presence even
if on a screen in a hotel room.

Step Two: Select the Right Options

Decide just what is critical to the success of your meeting and select
the telecommunications options to deliver these critical functions.

Ralph knew that for him to achieve the objectives he sought from
his meeting, everyone had to be there. The participants did not
have to see each other, they just needed to hear the word directly
from the boss that there were important moves afoot. On the other
hand, the studio press agent knew that the stars' presence was
needed to make his conference a success. They had to be seen, if
not in the flesh then on the screen as they were in the movies.

One-way video, two-way audio teleconferencing is becoming increasingly popular for presenting a new product to a nationwide
sales force, for stockholders' meetings, and for the President and
Vice-President to keep in touch with party leaders and encourage
campaign contributions. After all, everyone wants to see the President and he cannot be expected to leave Washington whenever
called on by a state party chairman.

Consider what you might need in order to coordinate your staff
away from the main office. As your business grows, it could become very profitable to locate key managers with small staffs closer
to your client. On the other hand, if you are spread out in a large

building or industrial complex, teleconferencing might be beneficial. Teleconferencing frees you from the constraints of geography.

Step Three: Know How to Purchase or Lease

Select teleconferencing systems and equipment for flexibility and cost. Consider leasing rather than purchasing so that you can always get the latest equipment. Teleconferencing costs can vary from simply the telephone charges you incur when you audio teleconference office to office to the costs of satellite transponder time and studio facilities, including directors, scriptwriters, camera operators, and more for a video conference. Table 14.2 offers a quick guide to teleconferencing costs.

Teleconferencing is a rapidly developing field. New systems and equipment appear almost monthly. A great many systems are designed to meet specific needs of firms installing major facilities. Consequently, there are numerous consultants, newsletters, and a few organizations at your disposal. A timely reference guide to the latest information on equipment, systems, and services can be found in *Definitive Buyer's Guide to Teleconferencing Products and Services* (Telespan, 50 West Palm Street, Altadena, CA 91001).

There is no reason why a single assemblage of technologies should be able to meet all of your teleconferencing needs. Select technologies that suit your needs, even if it means having more than one system in your office. Indeed, your telephone already provides you with an audio teleconferencing capability and, for all practical purposes, your teleconferencing services are leased rather than owned. All you pay is the telephone charges for the parties with whom you teleconference. And if you decide to expand your telephone system by means of the intelligent telephones we described in Chapter 4 and the PBX of Chapter 6, you have significantly added to the degree to which you can personally control your internal teleconferencing arrangements.

With the modern PBX and associated intelligent telephones, you have the beginnings of an enhanced audio teleconferencing system to which you can add computer conferencing and slow-scan video conferencing. You can do this as needed, in modular fashion, learning as you go. One good reason for growing into your teleconferencing needs in modular fashion is that you are not so technologically dependent if part of the system should malfunction. As you grow, you have more options (audio, video, and two-way) to depend on.

Table 14.2. Quick Guide to Teleconferencing Costs

Teleconferencing Option	Cost Components
Audio	
Office-to-office	Communications tariff (per minute)
	Speaker phones (optional)
Conference room	Communications tariff (per minute)
	Conference bridge
	Omnidirectional microphone
	Multiple speakers
	Acoustical preparation of room
Enhanced audio	Conference room (see above)
	Facsimile and communications Tariff (per minute)
	Text processing
	Personal computer
	Telewriting or electric blackboard
	Integrating controls
	Installation and maintenance
Video—full motion	Conference room (see above)
	Studio lighting
	Video cameras
	Video switches
	Audio/video master control
	Video monitors and/or large screen
	Projection system
	Video communications tariffs, cable, microwave, or satellite
	Installation and maintenance
	Facility director
Video—slow speed	Conference room (see above)
	Video monitors
	Slow-scan video system
Computer	Communications tariffs (per minute)
	Personal computer or communicating computer terminal, communicating word processor

Step Four: Invest in Implementation and Training

Getting the most out of your teleconferencing investments requires careful planning for installation and implementation, and it requires training. Before you invest too heavily in teleconferencing, get some experience. It is not wise to ask your staff to evaluate the potential benefits of something they haven't seen or tried. No matter how good your imagination is, reading about teleconferencing is no substitute for the real thing. Furthermore, over the past decade, there has been much misinformation about teleconferencing, ranging from ecstatic success stories to frightening failures; they could mislead you and your staff.

You might consider beginning with audio conferencing by way of the public switched telephone network. Plan several of your monthly staff meetings by teleconference and ask the conference operator to set it up for you. In that way you and your staff, both in your office as well as those in remote locations, will see how you like it. You'll have the basis for realistic evaluations. You can then learn from your own experiences and make better choices of the technology mix you need for teleconferencing—for example, whether you should add facilities for slow-scan video, for computer conferencing, or fax.

Another way to see teleconferencing in action is to ask for a demonstration from one of the providers of teleconferencing services. More than likely, they can arrange for you and your staff to see the system and even try it out at one of their operating installations.

Just as word processing and other information technologies alter office politics and office behavior so will teleconferencing. You cannot simply drop it into your office or company accompanied by directives that it be used to save money and expect it to be greeted with smiles. You will want your staff to recognize that teleconferencing is a telecommunication system that will make their work more productive, solve some of their troublesome traveling problems, and generally make their jobs more pleasurable.

Make your staff part of the solution by bringing them into the planning process. Involve them in your deliberations by inviting their opinions about what's wrong with their present way of doing their job and what they are learning about teleconferencing. You will have to set aside office space for your teleconferencing system and, as you know, whenever offices are shaken up, people get nervous. Involve your staff in planning for the locations and operation of the system. After all, it's the staff who will have to do the job, so they often appreciate being involved in the planning. An experienced staff can become your experts in expanding your teleconferencing capabilities. Perhaps there are venturesome people on your staff who will join you early on in adopting teleconferencing. If so, take advantage of their enthusiasm and they will spread it through your office.

You can expect early problems and some considerable trial and error in getting the system operating as you want it to. Indeed, you should adapt an attitude of experimentation during the early stages in the use of your teleconferencing systems and do not look for dramatic productivity or cost reductions too early.

Choose a supplier who will work with you in the installation and debugging of the system. Make sure your purchase agreement supports your system for a considerable period of time. Nothing is worse for generating confidence in any new office system than for it to sit idle while waiting for the service team to arrive.

No matter what type of conferencing system you are installing, do it in a manner that fits into your office style. The authors worked with their first teleconferencing system in the office of a small but highly profitable software firm, where people were scattered over what seemed like a warehouse, working in their shirtsleeves when the weather was cool and without shirts when the weather was hot. The informality of the office could be translated effectively into an easygoing conference style. If your office style is formal and your meetings are held around a formal conference table, then your teleconferencing facility should be installed in the same style. The objectives are to adapt and adopt teleconferencing quickly so that the payoffs you seek are quickly obtained.

Teleconferencing system providers will sometimes offer introductory training in the operation of the system. But, generally, it will be your responsibility to train your staff to use the system. Users with whom we have consulted report that the best training is use, and that many of the warnings and caveats about the kinds of meetings that are better or worse for this or that form of teleconferencing seem to disappear as people adapt the system to their own special style.

Step Five: Know How to Plan Conferences

Teleconferencing is a new and different way to manage so prepare for your teleconferences carefully; don't take risks because it seems easier; sometimes it isn't.

For example, audio is easy only if it is well done. Often you can stomach a fuzzy picture, but poor sound is almost unbearable. (Did you know that the human ear is more sensitive than the eye?) If grumbling under your breath is the way you show disapproval in a face-to-face meeting, realize that in an audio conference it may sound like furniture shuffling. You will have to speak more slowly, more distinctly, and perhaps more expressively in order to get your points across in an audio conference.

Teleconferencing, even video teleconferencing, does not particularly simulate face-to-face meetings. Teleconferencing is best thought of as another mode for communication, a special type of meeting in itself. The rules are different for a teleconference than for a face-to-face meeting.

Teleconferences are likely to be both shorter than face-to-face meetings and somewhat more formal and structured. If personal contact is your trademark, you might want to reconsider teleconferencing as a way of doing business. But if you do decide to teleconference, you need to set clear meeting objectives and come prepared with a tight agenda. You might find this style of management suits you even better.

Status and etiquette are as important in a teleconference as in a face-to-face meeting. If someone has to travel to a studio for a conference, who is it going to be? If you called the meeting and the participants have to travel, you will be seen as ''in charge.'' Is this the image you want to project? Or do you want your client to feel that you have organized the conference in order to attend more rapidly to his or her needs, even if the client has to ''meet'' you at some distant conference room? Audio conferences, like the telephone, are very democratic; everyone can be heard and even the shy often speak up.

Step Six: Evaluate

Regularly evaluate your teleconferencing activities so you can always have ideas for improvement. Chances are that you decided to use teleconferencing in order to reduce travel costs. Cost reduction is difficult to demonstrate in detail, yet most systems are purchased or leased for this purpose. If cost-reduction is your goal, then carefully plan for it—make it a corporate policy to substitute teleconferencing for travel where cost-savings merit the decision. Then evaluate the results.

There are, of course, other benefits of teleconferencing that you should be watching for and determining if, indeed, you are achieving them. Consider these:

Are you gathering more information faster?

Are you expanding your information sources?

Are you getting faster responses to your instructions?

Are your face-to-face meetings more efficient because you plan for them with one or more teleconferences?

Are your business trips shorter because you prepare for them more efficiently via one or more teleconferences?

Have you resolved emergencies faster, since you have been using teleconferencing?

Have your meetings been more productive because you have been able to have the right people on call by teleconferencing?

And look out for these problems:

Are more meetings being held by teleconferencing because "it's so easy"?

Has there been a feeling of growing social isolation among your remote staff members because so few face-to-face meetings are now being held?

Has there been a growing feeling of greater control from the center, from headquarters, and, consequently, a loss of confidence and morale in your field staff? Do you find your staff now waiting for your orders rather than acting on their own, as they did before teleconferencing? Remember, telecommunications can both increase or decrease control, as well as centralize or decentralize your operation.

Are you so dependent on teleconferencing that a recent disruption of telephone services left you helpless? Have you become vulnerable to technology?

15

TELECOMMUTING

WILSON Q. WORKS AT HOME AND LOVES IT

Wilson Q. is a very successful market analyst who stopped going into his firm's downtown office every day of the week more than 10 years ago. He was one of the early telecommuters, people who work at home at least part of their work week. He found he could just as well work with his clients on the telephone from his quiet home office, indeed, better than in the firm's office where he was always interrupted. However, he had to visit the main office on the other days in order to get some of the latest quotes that had come off the tape. Today, he has a personal computer at home, communicates with a number of databases that are online (see Chapter 12, Teleresearching), and works at home 3 days a week, doing even better than he did before.

Wilson Q. is one among many professionals, academics, consultants, and managers who find working at home periodically highly productive and nonthreatening. On the other hand, there are those among that group who fear that working at home too often may leave them out of the all-important personal networks at work thereby threatening their promotional possibilities.

If you are not already spending a day now and then working at home, have you given serious thought to how you might benefit from taking periodic advantage of that option? Have you given any thought to how it might benefit both you and your fellow managers and professionals if that option were available to them? Also there may be new valuable employees available to you if you took advantage of talented workers who, for one reason or another, had to work at, or closer to, their homes.

WHAT IS TELECOMMUTING?

Telecommuting is the word originally coined to describe the use of computers and telecommunications systems to enable you to work at home. Recently the term has been used more broadly to define the substitution of telecommunications for transportation, and for working in a satellite office closer to home as well as at home with or without computers.

Some individuals are enthusiastic about this different kind of work place activity. Hardly a month goes by without a newspaper special feature or Sunday supplement article about this new lifestyle. Many people already do some of their work at home at least part of the time. It is not unusual to reason that the time you save by not driving or riding is time that you can devote directly to your work, in addition to other benefits. Executives take work from their offices to the relative quiet of their homes not only for evening and weekend work, but may even spend a day or so a month at home during the normal work week catching up on their endless paperwork. For those days the executive has traded off commuting to the office for working at home.

Telecommunications still preserves some of the vital links to the office. For example, you can call your office to dictate a memorandum or letter or ask for a teleconference with members of your staff. With your personal computers you can send mail by way of the several electronic mail networks (see Chapter 13, Telemailing) or upload documents to the office word processor or mainframe for final preparation and distribution by way of their local area networks (see Chapter 8, Local Area Networks). As an executive you can use telecommunications to enhance your work away from the office, one of the key benefits of telecommuting.

Obviously, telecommuting is not limited to managers, executives, professionals, and academics. Clerical and secretarial work can often be performed out of the office. Men or women at home, either for reason of choice, young children, or physical limitations, have found in the telecommuting option a source of money otherwise not available to them. Software programmers have been known to favor the quiet of their homes for their lonely work. Indeed, IBM provides facilities to enable many of their programmers to work at home, at least part of the time.

WHAT HAPPENS WHEN THE BOSS WORKS AT HOME?

The Experience Is Mostly Positive

The chances are you already take your work home with you on some evenings and weekends. If you are an occasional home-worker, you probably find those moments very productive and rewarding. And you feel little guilt because you have kept up with your work schedule. If this work-away time is so valuable, why not regularly schedule work at home several days a month? You need not be out of touch; your calls can be screened by your secretary and forwarded to your home. For the self-employed manager–consultant with a part-time secretary, you can program your office telephone to call-forward your calls to your home. You can arrange to screen the forwarded calls before you answer. Even if you do not subscribe to these telephone services, you can use your answering machine to listen in to the caller, then decide which calls you will answer now and which you will postpone to a later time.

By way of your personal computer, you can access office information resources if you are preparing reports and need that vital data from the company's electronic files. Via telemail you can address questions to your staff without tying up your time playing telephone tag or waiting on the telephone for them to obtain the information. The intelligent telephones and PBXs discussed in Chapters 4 and 5 are your home-to-office management links. Tele-banking, researching, mailing, and conferencing via your personal computer enhance your management abilities from your home.

Periodic work-at-home days need not in any way harm your managerial effectiveness. There is no evidence that managers who telecommute lose touch with their staffs. To the contrary, the electronic message or telephone call to a staff member from the boss's home is often more effective in getting results than the same message delivered by the boss in the office. Indeed, you are likely to be a more creative manager if you extend those rewarding evenings and weekends into several work-at-home days each month.

A Few Negatives

Of course, there are some problems associated with working at home. Relative to being removed from the office environment, the main complaint is the loss of immediate personal contact for a critical conversation. There is also the loss of opportunity for small-talk or chance encounters that sometimes prove productive.

There are also complaints that mixing work with home life has its shortcomings. One is that if there is family at home to compete for your attention, it is difficult to work without feeling guilty one way or another. (In that case, it is helpful to have a separate study or office at home and an agreement that you are not "home from work" but "home to work" for the day.) Another is that your feeling of your home as a refuge or place to relax may be eroded by mixing in too much work. After all, you do need some environment where you can feel relaxed. Having your computer staring at you can be intimidating.

Most of these negatives are a matter for individuals to weigh against the advantages of telecommuting. Different individual preferences and family situations may ultimately be the main factors in your decision about working at home.

HOW YOUR FIRM CAN BENEFIT FROM TELECOMMUTING

Who Can Work At Home?

Candidates for working at home fall into two groups: (1) professional and technical and (2) secretarial and clerical workers. Tasks within these classifications do not require being on location at all times or face-to-face contact with others at all times. "Work-alone" jobs are especially well suited to alternative-site working arrangements.

Professional work has typically been information work and will be increasingly so. Likely occupations include engineers, lawyers and paralegal personnel, computer system analysts and programmers, writers, editors, accountants, sales persons for services and products, real estate brokers, financial analysts, stocks and bond merchants, insurance workers, and many types of consultant. Individuals in such occupations can work independently of others;

hence they are good candidates for working at home or at some location other than a main downtown office, such as a satellite facility closer to their homes.

Clerical occupations for at home or satellite office work include general office clerks, secretaries, typists, bookkeepers and accountants, auditors, data inputters, and coders.

Improving Productivity Through Telecommuting

If properly managed, your professionals working at home or closer to home can perform efficiently. You can also expect carefully chosen clerks, bookkeepers, even secretaries and typists, working either at home or closer to home, to be as efficient and just as satisfied (or more satisfied) than office workers. Some examples:

One of the more famous work-at-home projects, the Blue Cross/ Blue Shield ''Cottage Keyers'' in South Carolina, has demonstrated that more claims are processed with fewer errors by the remote workers than by those working in the home office.

Officials of Mountain Bell report that their training course writers working at home prepare more courses and do it faster at home than do course writers at the headquarters offices. This results in faster processing of students through training and on the job.

A major insurance company found that adjusters and inspectors worked as effectively out of their homes as they did out of the regional offices, visiting these offices no more than one or, at most, two days a week.

Many consultants regularly work out of their home or on the road, making telecommuting a regular way of life.

Increasing the Pool of Talented Workers Through Telecommuting

Providing alternative work sites closer to your employees' homes as well as allowing staff to work at home can make those otherwise unavailable secretaries and professionals available to you. Often making these work location options available will provide you with motivated workers. Consider, for example, a secretary who left the office to raise her family, but who now would love to get involved again, even if it's from home. Many persons ''at home'' could have productive and well-paid work opportunities if only you could reach them and they could reach you from their homes. Past experience has shown that this pool of talent is often highly skilled and productive. For some employees the ability to periodically choose to remain at home offers opportunities to share household burdens with partners and improve family relationships. The increased flexibility with which they could deal with their lives can make for happier and more productive employees.

Cutting Costs Through Telecommuting

If some portions of your operations can be performed by people working at home, you may save office space and with that heating and cooling costs. With growing congestion on the roads leading to downtown offices, avoiding the journey several times a week saves employee time (on the average this amounts to one hour per day for the roundtrip journey) and fuel as well as parking costs. Your employees would also save wear and tear on clothing and the costs of eating out during the workday. Professionals might well enjoy the ability to concentrate in an environment of reduced work stress, while secretaries and clerks could appreciate the reduced supervision under which they would work. All this could lead to more satisfied personnel when raise or union contract negotiations come around.

WHAT WILL TELECOMMUTING COST YOU?

The benefits of telecommuting do not come free. Your remote secretary may require either a communicating word processor or personal computer and modem. The communicating costs, telephone bills for the link or links between office, home, or satellite office could be an additional charge. Some workers may market their work-at-home services by offering to provide their own equipment. Also, remote work does not always require telecommunications.

If you choose to set up a satellite office—that is, an office that is closer to where some of your staff lives—it will mean additional floor space. More often than not, this space will be much less expensive than your downtown space. But you may not be able to reallocate all of your remote worker's space at your main office. Many employees who chose to work at or near home will often want to keep their offices or desks at your main office. But you should try to work out a scheme for sharing space among the remote workers, perhaps flexibly scheduling their in-office time so they can make use of a common space.

Be prepared to provide extra documentation and instructions for remote workers who will not now have managers or fellow workers to supervise or assist them. Remember that the telephone and telemail can be of great help for providing assistance when needed. When the tasks performed at remote sites are closely linked to activities at main offices, such as completing sales and other transactions, you might encounter some coordination problems. But this, too, is likely to disappear as more and more transactions are carried out online or on the network.

MANAGING THE TELECOMMUTERS

Your biggest challenge is learning how to manage workers at remote sites over long periods of time. Beware of becoming isolated from them or thinking that you are isolated because they are not in the same office or building with you. With your busy travel schedule, how often do you see some of your staff now?

Don't fall into the trap of questioning the loyalty of employees because you do not see them everyday. You do see their work, and with modern telecommunications you will be in as much voice and data contact with them (perhaps even video contact) as you desire. If many of your staff are part-timers and working at home or at a satellite facility, you might have difficulty with their identities when salary review time comes around. There is an added responsibility of maintaining contact, perhaps by one or two social events that will bring them together. But there is the telephone conference and the telephone itself, and we have seen that managers soon learn to use these telecommunications tools as effectively as they do face-to-face communications. The increasing number of telecommunicating options becoming available to you will enable you to overcome this difficulty and at best it will not last for long.

Remote work does not mean that you never see your employees.

As we noted previously, most workers do not want to disappear entirely; they want the option of working away from the main office and still being a member of the team.

Employees are very well aware of the danger of being forgotten or left out of their peer network. Professional and clerical remote workers, part-time and full-time, feel that social isolation is the most pressing and anxiety producing problem they have when working at home. They fear that long periods of isolation from their peers and supervisors will cost them promotions. If you wish to have the benefits of telecommuting not only for yourself but for your staff you must be sensitive to these social costs and make provisions to overcome them. The aforementioned social events may be a way to deal with this difficulty. Clerical workers at home or in neighborhood offices are afraid of being paid by the "piece," having no benefits, and certainly no opportunity for collective bargaining. Consequently, unless you counter these fears you are likely to have high turnover, and instead of saving money you will be spending a great deal more constantly training new workers.

Finally, since so many of these workers may turn out to be women there is a growing belief that women may, once again, be segregated to working at home. Consequently, you should work within the guidelines of the Fair Labor Standards Act of 1938. This Act defines clerical work and makes certain that the "sweatshops" do not return. Unions are becoming more vigilant and there is nothing to be gained by running afoul of them.

SIX RULES FOR MANAGING TELECOMMUTERS

1. *Telecommunications Is the Key to the Productive Use of Telecommuting.* Make certain you have installed what you believe is necessary for keeping in touch with your remote workers and for getting work to them and work from them. This does not always mean a computer communications network. An intelligent telephone, your cellular mobile telephone for you to reach them while on the move, and surface mail or third party electronic messaging may do quite well (see Chapter 13, Telemailing).

2. *Select Your Remote Workers Carefully.* It takes a certain amount of maturity and self-control to work away from peers. Remote workers are usually older and more experienced workers, having spent some part of their working lives in positions where they were

on their own. Assign or hire someone with whom you have previously worked or has previously worked for you.

3. *Select Carefully the Work to Be Done.*   Not all work lends itself to remote accomplishment. Work that can be done with little or no contact with others is, clearly, best suited. And work that requires a very high degree of concentration with as little interruption as possible is a good candidate for doing in the home. That is why computer programming is often seen as the model for remote work and programmers tend to be nontalkative loners. So much of information based work can be done "by telephone" or on the network, it may not be necessary to limit the nature of the work to stand-alone tasks. After all, a report can be drafted in the office and sent via an electronic mail network to an editor who can prepare the report for final typing and sent via the network to the typist who may be in still another location.

4. *Do Not Isolate Your Remote Workers.*   Have your remote workers visit the office now and then. Provide them with desk and office space so when they come they feel welcome and important. You should also have personnel visit them, especially if they are working in one of your ad hoc satellite locations. Ensure that they have excellent telecommunications access to you.

5. *Do Not Penalize Workers for Not Being in the Office.*   This is perhaps your most challenging task. Many remote workers may be part-time workers and their pay scales and benefits reflect this. It is easy to take undue advantage of someone who needs the work and cannot come into the office every day but is willing to work at home. But if you do, you can be certain that in a short time the employee will leave you. The rewards of the remote workers must be seen as being fair both to your regular main office staff as well as to the remote worker.

6. *If Possible Establish a Satellite Branch Rather than Depend on Home Workers.*   Social isolation is the enemy of the remote worker. An informal setting for more than one person, where a feeling of community can be established, will do wonders to alleviate isolation. If this is located appropriately, it might be possible to attract workers who otherwise are not available to you. It is also a location where you might want to establish a part-time manager.

7. *Do Not Expect to Escape from the Congestion of the Downtown Business District.* It is true that the telephone has done wonders for decentralizing business activities away from the crowded downtown central business districts. And we can expect that new telecommunications as discussed will increase the migration from these areas. But you as an executive will always want to be near your peers, near to the bankers on whom you depend for capital, and close to potential clients. The downtown area will continue to be the place for those meetings that require face-to-face contact, the meeting ground for those executives who are willing to pay prices for space in order to take advantage of the special benefits of interpersonal communication.

16
TELEMARKETING

WHAT'S DISTINCTIVE ABOUT TELEMARKETING?

Personal Selling

Virginia, marketing director of a West Coast textbook company, has just been appointed a vice president, a promotion openly acknowledged to reflect her restructuring of the company's marketing program. She had innovatively introduced telemarketing *in her company.*

Traditionally, textbook companies have promoted their list to "faculty adopters" through a combination of advertising, convention booths, direct mail, and the most effective yet costly practice of having "reps" who visit schools to engage in traditional face-to-face selling. Like many marketing executives, Virginia found her business edging up to the "80–20" rule—that is, 80 percent of her business was coming from 20 percent of her customers. In fact, the remaining 80 percent of her territory had been in the red for the last few years and her challenge was to remedy the situation. But better than remedy it, she converted it into a profit-making sector by changing the marketing strategy.

Her first step was to replace rep visits to marginally profitable campuses with personally oriented telephone calls. The result was rewarding. She was able to maintain the same general level of sales but cut the cost of selling by about a factor of 10. To this program, Virginia added a campaign to stir up inactive accounts by direct mail with follow up phone calls. The results increased her number of active accounts and gave her marketing feedback on reasons why others remained inactive (courses dropped, faculty changes, etc.).

But Virginia's "outbound" telemarketing program did not stop there. She encouraged her reps to keep in closer touch with their best clients by phone, and she launched a major effort to build up an "inbound " telemarketing program where prospective adopters call in for information or orders. No ad is placed or direct mail piece posted without the company's inbound 800 number clearly visible and a well trained staff ready to answer it. Many of their best clients have complimented the company for offering this service!

Virginia is using modern telecommunications for *personal selling*. It is a strategy for customer contact, research, service, inbound order-taking, as well as outbound calling for sales. It is the most rapidly growing method of marketing. Some estimates place the percentage of telephone-based sales at 50 percent by the 1990s as compared with 15 percent at the close of the 1970s. Also, telemarketing strategies are applicable to such nonbusiness applications as fundraising, employee recruiting, or locating volunteers for a civic organization. Although new technologies and related services have greatly contributed to the opportunities for telemarketing, it remains a highly intensive *managerial* undertaking.

Is this just plain old telephone solicitation with a fancy name? Although the unwelcome ring is still around, the most effective telemarketing programs are like Virginia's. They emphasize personal and continuing contact with known customers or individuals who have requested information rather than the canvassing of "cold" contacts. One final note regards the use of automatic dialing devices and recordings for sales messages. Avoid this unless you have little regard for your company's future (or the public's patience).

Six Advantages of Telemarketing

1. *Reduce Your Sales Cost.*   As in Virginia's example, a telemarketing program can visibly reduce the cost of marketing your product. A current rule of thumb is that the typical face-to-face sales call may average $200 or more as compared with "outbound" telemarketing calls, which may average $15 to $20. Remember, too, that

costs of salaries, travel, and lodging have constantly increased over the last decade, while long distance telephone rates have fallen. One implication of this is that some accounts cannot remain profitable via traditional sales practices. Further, the public as well as buyers in business organizations are increasingly familiar with "800" number usage. "Inbound" telemarketing reduces costs still more.

2. *Increase Personal Rapport with Customers.* You know from your own experience that the telephone is second only to face-to-face communication for "personal" communication. For any potential customer, telemarketing is a possible alternative to direct sales calls, especially where you estimate that the cost of the personal visit is likely to outweigh the sale potential. Also for the valued customer, follow-up calls will keep the client "warm" for additional personal visits. So, too, can the telephone reawaken a potentially valuable client. Calling for an appointment will not only cut down waiting time but can also increase your sensitivity to your client's "need" or purchasing cycle.

3. *Augment Other Marketing Programs.* In the past decade, much of the growth of telemarketing has been to enhance the convenience and ultimate impact of direct mail as well as media (i.e., magazine, newspaper, radio, and television) advertising. The popular "800" order or information number is now an established business practice in both types of promotion. The companies that profit most from this practice are those who coordinate an effective response to customer call-ins, or "inbound" services. Also, an outbound telephone call will often be an effective follow-up to a direct mail campaign, and the mailing gives the salesperson a reason for calling. These activities will further contribute to the reduction in the number of "cold contacts" that may prove expensive in face-to-face selling.

4. *Expand Your Sales Potential.* Because the telephone offers the opportunity for immediate interaction with a customer, it creates an opportunity for expansion of sales in the transaction. For example, effective telemarketers are often able to increase orders by an "enhancer" (volume discounts, premiums, deferred payments) or by "cross-selling" (recommending related products). Telephone contacts also provide an effective method for test marketing new products or marketing strategies. Finally, telephone conversation is

second only to face-to-face selling as a means for encouraging customers to act immediately—to place their orders *now*.

5. *Gather Market Information.* Telemarketing offers the opportunity to rapidly test the customers' interest in new products, or their responsiveness to price cuts or volume buying advantages of existing ones. Because the customer is in a position to provide immediate feedback on your product, telemarketing is a valuable source of information on competing products or their prices. You will almost always be gathering information on reasons for not buying a competitive product or service, an impossibility with media promotions.

6. *Gain New Flexibilities.* A telemarketing campaign can be changed on a day's notice, which is impossible to do if your marketing campaign depends solely on people on the road, direct mail, or media. For example, if you find that the market for one of your products seems to be expanding, you can literally change your telemarketing techniques within the hour and follow up just as quickly with increases on the production line. Your telemarketers are always getting feedback from their calls and feedback to your sales themes and approaches. If you find that your sales strategies do not work or if you want to try a different approach, you can experiment and revise them until you hit on the most effective one. You can then revise your media mail campaigns to follow suit.

MANAGEMENT OF TELEMARKETING

Planning

Your first step in developing or refining a telemarketing plan is to consider how this type of marketing will specifically serve your needs. Ask yourself the following questions:

1. Will telemarketing be my sole marketing strategy?
2. Am I going to use telemarketing to support or eventually replace face-to-face selling?
3. Will I use telemarketing techniques as a follow-up to direct mail or media advertising (e.g., 800 call-back numbers)?

4. Will I use it to qualify clients as a basis for direct sales calls?

5. To what degree will I use telemarketing as a basis for testing new product appeal, sales strategies, or pricing?

Answers to these questions will not only suggest the type of overall marketing plan you will develop or modify but also the relative amount of investment in personnel, equipment, and their management in order to initiate your program. Bear in mind, too, that telemarketing can take a wide variety of forms as well as investments. It can range from a multimillion dollar investment in staff, telephone equipment, computers, 800 lines, associated media advertising, and management costs for a multimillion dollar firm, to a campaign for a very small business where the owner wishes to test certain clients or markets by personally making telephone contacts.

How do you get started? In most areas of the country, you can get a wide range of advice on telemarketing—not only equipment but sales strategies and employee training—from your local telephone account executive. You may have noticed in the last several years that the former Bell system regional companies (as well as some others) have actively advertised programs for telemarketing. These services include seminars for managerial and staff training. You will also want to discuss your needs with telemarketing consultants, most of whom you will be able to locate through your telephone company, marketing or advertising firms, as well as occasional advertisements found in business publications. There is an excellent magazine that can serve as a source of information on strategies, equipment, procedures, and innovations. It is:

Telemarketing
Technology Marketing Building
17 Park Street
Norwalk, CT 06851
(800/243-6002)
(203/846-2029 in Connecticut)

Once you have defined your objectives, you will be in a position to know the type of staff, working environment, and management required for your operation. Table 16.1 is a checkoff list (offered by the Pacific Bell company) for getting started, or reorganizing your efforts, for telemarketing.

Table 16.1 Checkoff List for Telemarketing[a]

Conduct time and account analysis
Review analysis and segment accounts
Establish goals and objectives
Review physical facilities and communication needs
Establish job description
Develop organization structure and supervisory relationships
Develop compensation plan
Initiate internal awareness program
Initiate recruiting program
Interview and hire personnel
Initiate training program (selling skills, product knowledge)
Initiate external (customer) awareness program
Review procedures and forms
Initiate implementation test
Review implementation test
Mail customer announcement letter
Initiate telemarketing inside sales program

[a]Courtesy of Pacific Bell.

Equipment and Services

Obviously if you're going to initiate a large number of toll calls, you will want some type of wide area of dialing or discount service. Although telephone account executives are a valuable source of information on their own company's services, you will want to examine alternative long distance "outbound" services (e.g., MCI or Sprint). Also, you should look into remote call forwarding ("RCF") for inbound telemarketing. This is where an individual calls a local number and the call is transferred to your headquarters.

If your telemarketing operation is mainly "inbound," you will almost always want to establish an 800 number for your operation. This is done through your telephone company account executive. All the evidence shows that an 800 number in a media advertisement or direct mail material, or simply made available to clients, is well worth the investment.

One detail you may have noticed with 800 numbers is that they are frequently listed along with an area code required if the call is made within the state where the company is located. It is possible to acquire one 800 number that operates within your state also, but the expense will be greater. A single 800 number, beyond being more convenient for the client, will keep your company from acquiring a regional image. (If you are selling supplies of some fast turnaround item, a regional image may discourage customers from other parts of the country.)

You will also want to consider the number of calls that you will be able to handle simultaneously. This requires not only extra lines so your incoming calls can be switched to separate phones, but the additional personnel to answer them.

At the minimum you should invest in handsets that are not only comfortable for continuous use but leave the operator's hands free for writing or handling documents. Typical among your choices is the "Star" set which has light weight headphones and speaker tube. These are available through most any business-oriented telephone vendor.

For larger scale operations, you will want efficient switching equipment so callers' incoming calls can be quickly routed to a staff member and placed on hold if necessary, as well as equipment that allows for rapid dialing or interfacing with computer phone number files for automatic dialing (see Chapter 4. The Intelligent Telephone). There are even special answering machines for efficient handling of off-hour calls or for taking orders. All such equipment, as well as systems that allow for monitoring calls by a supervisor, is available through specialized vendors that you can reach through consultants or publications like the aforementioned magazine.

Work Environment

If telemarketing is to be a serious part of your business, you should set aside appropriate space—a pleasant work environment for your personnel. Almost all telemarketing consultants will tell you that personnel who staff a telemarketing operation will perform at a much higher level of efficiency if they are not also simultaneously involved in additional duties. (But it is sometimes desirable to divide their work day between calling and another type of duty.)

Work space should be separate from other parts of your organization. One ideal configuration is a room divided by "office landscaping" into individual carrels for the staff members. Each carrel should be three-sided and sufficiently high so as to screen out coworkers. In short, you will want an environment where your callers can give full attention to their business. Seating should be particularly comfortable, and the desk a proper height so that the time spent sitting, and concentrating on clients, does not result in eye strain or backache.

If you want to have the best performance from your telemarketers, you must design a schedule that varies periods of intense activity with periods that are relatively pleasurable and relaxing. There is a high rate of "burnout" in telemarketers, and you do not want to lose them just when you have invested in their experience. You can prevent burnout by providing a pleasant work environment and schedule, provisions for those who smoke as well as for those who do not, and time for coffee breaks and other refreshments. Be especially vigilant to strongly discourage smoking, eating, or drinking while on the telephone, all of which can be very distracting to a listener.

Increasingly, more advanced telemarketing operations are furnishing personnel with computer terminals or small computers for holding "scripts," taking notes, and some for automatic dialing. As with other specialized equipment, you can obtain information on these from telemarketing vendors. However, even if you are a relatively small telemarketing operation, you should consider ways that personal computers can be configured to facilitate the operation.

The telemarketing work environment is also one that lends itself to possible placement in the worker's home (as so-called home work). If you can manage the necessary performance control of your personnel, you might consider this alternative, although there are special considerations for equipment and management (see Chapter 15, Telecommuting).

Personnel

Frankly, it takes a particular type of personality not only to be successful but to endure the job of selling by phone. Beyond this, an important factor is the "voice personality" an individual generates over the telephone, based on the quality of the voice and the patterns of speech. Individuals with heavily regional or ethnic accents are not as successful in telemarketing as people whose speech characteristics do not immediately denote a particular image. There are also the subtle effects of voice qualities and manner that will make one person sound energetic or friendly and another bored, distant or aloof in a telephone conversation. Consider using the questionnaire shown in Figure 16.1 as a basis for gauging voice personality.

As the proof in the performance, one tip is that when you or your manager hire individuals for telemarketing work, interview them first over the telephone. Their "voice image" is going to be far more important to you than their in-person one. If an individual's telephone performance puts you off at first, there is usually no sense in trying to retrain; it will not be worth the investment. On the other hand, if there are only one or two characteristics that are bothersome about a person, usually these can be handled by training.

Beyond voice personality, you will want to be sure that the individuals have the capability to learn about your product or service so they can be fluent when answering questions, and so that you can depend on them to always present your product in the most positive and informative manner. Some of this is predictable from job interviews, but you will almost always want to sample an employee's performance. Special phone equipment provides for this, or you can have a supervisor make a random inbound call for in-

Telephone Personality Evaluation Form

Place one check mark per scale*

1. The caller sounds:

         positive ---- : ---- : ---- : ---- : ---- : ---- : ---- negative
           alert ---- : ---- : ---- : ---- : ---- : ---- : ---- lazy
          happy ---- : ---- : ---- : ---- : ---- : ---- : ---- grumpy
       educated ---- : ---- : ---- : ---- : ---- : ---- : ---- uneducated
         careful ---- : ---- : ---- : ---- : ---- : ---- : ---- careless
      courteous ---- : ---- : ---- : ---- : ---- : ---- : ---- rude
            calm ---- : ---- : ---- : ---- : ---- : ---- : ---- emotional
    trustworthy ---- : ---- : ---- : ---- : ---- : ---- : ---- untrustworthy

2. The caller's speech and language are:

          clear ---- : ---- : ---- : ---- : ---- : ---- : ---- unclear
      expressive ---- : ---- : ---- : ---- : ---- : ---- : ---- dull
        natural ---- : ---- : ---- : ---- : ---- : ---- : ---- unnatural
       pleasant ---- : ---- : ---- : ---- : ---- : ---- : ---- unpleasant

3. How much would I like to conduct business with the caller?
    very much ---- : ---- : ---- : ---- : ---- : ---- : ----not at all

*For each scale think of how what you are rating is described by one or the other of the adjectival opposites, then indicate this by placing your check mark somewhere between the two. If your feelings are about equal between the two adjectives, place your check mark in the center cell. These scales are taken by permission of the publisher from: Frederick Williams, *Executive Communication Power*. Englewood Cliffs, NJ: Prentice-Hall, 1983.

Figure 16.1.   Questionnaire for rating voice personality

formation. And there is also the ultimate evaluation—how well your product is sold.

Finally, telemarketing offers excellent job opportunities for handicapped or other homebound workers. In fact, you may benefit from seeking them out.

Training

Although telemarketing is one of the jobs that still can be learned "on the floor," there are numerous advantages in having a training program. Almost any person's telephone capabilities can be improved by training, even a modest amount. The problem is that the telephone is so frequently used in our society that most people never consider that they could improve on their abilities for projecting a more pleasant personality, sounding fluent and energetic, or being an attractive person to do business with. Especially important, too, are the tactics for making a sale—how to present a product, how to "close." There are also strategies for handling difficult personalities on the phone, especially hostility.

It is often said that telemarketers who are especially adept at sensing a customer's needs are "expert listeners." They have the ability to know when to let the customer talk, then how to incorporate that information into their sales appeals.

It is also critical that employees have a thorough knowledge of the products or services they are representing. Because the telephone is an interactive medium, employees can expect callers to ask questions and even to gauge the product in terms of the employee's enthusiasm over the telephone. Lack of employee knowledge is a problem that you may encounter when you hire third-party organizations to handle your telemarketing. Typically these employees are trained to say that they are only taking orders and they handle many products, therefore they cannot provide personal service to the caller. This almost always creates a negative image of your product.

In all, although you may train some employees directly "on the floor"—for example, by having them monitor calls made by experienced personnel—you will probably want to consider special training. A number of consulting services are available to help you with your training needs, but check them out with their clients before hiring them.

Evaluation and Incentives

Successful telemarketing, like the management of any sales activities, requires monitoring, evaluation, and the provision of highly visible incentives. A professional operation will require that employees keep a daily record of their calls, and that these be analyzed relative to sales or services that have been accomplished. Such data are then compiled in daily or weekly averages, then used as a basis for individual employee evaluations, distributing rewards, or setting new goals and establishing incentives to reach them. These activities are a never-ending part of the management of telemarketing. Some firms make occasional recordings (with permission, of course) of their telemarketers in action.

Incentives can take many forms, not just the rewards themselves but innovative conditions set for achieving them. For example, a prize can be given for the first or largest sale of the day, and another for the best weekly average. Or you might devise a bonus system that is calibrated by a rank ordering of the sales performance of all of the employees. If these goals are made explicit along with the record-keeping system, the effective manager can not only thoroughly evaluate the return of the telemarketing investment but constantly increase the effectiveness of the program.

Meetings Are Important

Well executed meetings are a key feature of telemarketing management. They are a valuable motivational strategy whereby callers can gain a sense of motivation and enthusiasm as a "team." Also, the shared experiences of handling difficult situations not only provide useful information for employees, but help to reduce negative feelings and stress because an individual learns that his or her problems are experienced by others.

You can use a meeting to demonstrate new scripts or sales strategies, even to set up role playing situations where different employees take the roles of callers who have various problems. Training can be a regular part of your meetings. You might introduce a specific topic each week, for example, how to increase cross-selling capabilities, how to handle complaints, or how to get to "yes" more effectively.

SALES STRATEGIES

Importance of Scripts

Basically, a script is either an outline or verbatim record of the language that you want your telemarketers to use when presenting different products or services, or in responding to inquiries or orders. Most scripts are "branched," meaning that the employee can use different statements depending on the types of request raised by the prospect. Scripts enable you to manage the quality control of employees' telephone interactions.

Consultants say that there is always a natural tendency for employees to want to avoid scripts. However, experience has shown that you will have much more control over the consistency of telephone transactions as well as the ability to introduce new content if you use scripts. Moreover, scripts can be developed, tested, refined, and constantly evaluated as they are used. They provide you with a basis for setting an accumulative program of improvement into operation. Although a well-trained writer can create material that aptly fits the oral form of telephone speech, it is usually best to work out scripts by speaking aloud, then to transcribe the key words and sentences.

One particularly effective format of scripts is to have them in a looseleaf notebook so that the main presentation is contained along with subscripts for handling different inquiries or complaints, or for suggestions on how to enhance the order of sales related products. The "closing" is particularly important in scripts because even some of the most experienced sales personnel can become so involved that the details of "asking for the business" are overlooked or slighted.

If you are using computers to record call information or to initiate calls, you might also use them to handle the script materials. With a little training it is very easy for an employee to "branch" between the parts of a script that are in a computer file. You want to make sure to constantly evaluate and improve your scripts.

Scripts are also an important tool for training new employees. You can directly show them the information you wish to be conveyed in their telephone interactions. This is much more precise than giving them general guidelines.

Qualities of Effective Scripts

Effective scripts are typically brief and to the point. They present your product or service in the best possible light and using crisp, direct, and visual language. And as the long-time sales adage says, a script "sells satisfaction." Scripts should also take particular advantage of the interactive quality of telephone conversations. That is, you can seek the particular needs of the client and then design your product or service message most specifically to those needs. *What's in it for me?* is the most important question you can answer for a customer.

Increased orders also evolve from the use of "enhancers" or those additional benefits that will invite a customer to increase his or her order. For example, the salesperson might suggest that a larger order or a continuing one will bring the advantages of a volume discount. Another enhancer is the use of premiums. For example, if a particular size order is made at this point, the customer could receive an additional product free of charge or at a sizable discount. Also, discounts can be carried over to other products so that if a larger order is made now, the customer can receive an additional 5 percent discount on those goods. These are all important options that can be located in scripts so as not to be overlooked by your sales personnel. Although sales personnel might naturally think of enhancers or cross-selling in outbound calling, scripts are especially effective for inbound applications. Rather than simply staffing your 800 number with "order takers," turn them into a sales force.

One final and important characteristic of scripts is that they emphasize the importance of closing the sale. Even among experienced telephone sales personnel, a presentation may get sufficiently sidetracked so that the direct move is not made to close the sale—to "ask for the business." Different closings can be tested and then incorporated later into the master script.

Some of the more detailed qualities of effective scripts include:

Language that is highly visual, that promotes imagery

Materials that are particularly interpretable from the customer's point of view

An offer that is revealed quickly and invitingly

Strategies for getting around hesitations or complaints

An exchange that seems personal as well as professional
Strategies for enhancing orders or for cross-selling

Scripts and associated training should also help your employees sense when they have reached a dead end with the client. This is not to say that the client should be cut off abruptly. But when it is clear that your product or service will not be desirable, it is best to terminate the interaction in a pleasant professional way, so that the time your employees invest will be directed to new client opportunities.

ARE YOU READY FOR "ONLINE" SELLING?

Although telemarketing is currently conducted over telephone networks, there is a new and growing practice of having clients link their personal computers via the telephone network to computer-based shopping services. Text displays show catalogs, invite questions, and allow for purchases to be made "online." These activities fit within the larger scope of what is known today as "video-text." Part of the future of telemarketing is surely involved in the expansion of videotext services. If you wish to see an example of these, read about the "Electronic Mall" or "Comp-U-Store" (Chapter 12, Teleresearching). You may wish to offer your products through a videotext shopping service or start your own "inbound" service. One great advantage is that it is not as employee intensive as telephone-based telemarketing.

17
TELETRAINING

A CRITICAL INVESTMENT

A major Midwestern R&D firm found only 2 of 16 special functions of a new "intelligent" telephone system being extensively used. Gauged relative to the costs of replacing the former phone installation, productivity had actually dropped 80 percent!

Training eventually solved this problem of underutilization, but it took attention and money. As we say so many places in this book, you cannot overlook the critical necessity of training personnel to use the new information technologies. Training is more than just operating a new PBX, mail system, or local area network; it is in *how you get your personnel to get the most out of its use.* In short, proper investments in training are what often give you that extra edge.

The new telecommunications offer a partial answer to your training needs. You can use telecommunications or related instructional materials to train people to effectively use information technologies. We call this "teletraining." Some examples described briefly in this chapter include:

Built-in training or assistance capabilities
"Help" or "800" numbers
"Online" computer assisted instruction

Instructional television
Electronic bulletin boards

OPPORTUNITIES FOR TELETRAINING

Built-In Training Aides

Many modern software-based telecommunications systems, such as telephone exchanges, intelligent telephones, various computer-based messaging systems, local area networks, database services, conferencing systems, and banking services, have a degree of training built into them. Features to look for include:

Tutorials. In addition to customary instruction books or programs, these provide step-by-step examples of common applications of the equipment or service. They may be in the form of special publications, or better yet, software components.

"Beginner" versus "Expert" command options. In many database services, for example, there are simple menus that you can follow to get your desired information. They give you a feel of the "territory," a sense of how the information is organized. But the same services may also have a set of "short-cut" commands that bypass menus and take you directly to your goal. You or your employees soon learn these commands almost by second nature as you grow familiar with the service.

Special templates. Perhaps you've seen them for intelligent telephones, special word processing or spreadsheet computer programs, or on facsimile machines. They are simple slip-on or paste-on templates that summarize basic commands, identify frequent uses of keys, or remind you of the sequence of an operation. There are also small "cheat-sheets" often provided to each user, small booklets that can be kept on the desk for easy referral.

Help files. Some software systems, especially where the application is computer-intensive, include entire sets of "help" files so that during any operation (e.g., sending electronic mail), you can stop momentarily and ask for assistance. In the better versions, the software will automatically provide the information for whatever operation you are currently engaged in; you need only press the "help" command. These systems can sometimes be used as a training tutorial.

"Help" or "800" Numbers

Not much need be said about the familiar 800 number for gaining help with equipment or service. But you should ask:

Does the vendor offer such support (and with an 800 number rather than a toll call)?

Do the hours of operation correspond to your work day?

Is the help line answered promptly and by knowledgeable personnel?

Are the personnel who answer apt to be courteous and encouraging to your employees? (In our experience, we often find that employees are intimidated by personnel who are impatient with their questions; this can be costly to you in terms of motivation.)

If help-line personnel cannot solve your problem on the spot, do they offer follow-up options?

Are there local offices from which service personnel can be dispatched?

In short, test any "help" service that is offered to you.

"Online" Computer-Assisted Instruction

Mainframe computers have been the basis for wide variety of educational applications since the 1960s. In the heyday of such applications, most instruction involved a direct wire linkage to terminals located in instructional laboratories. In addition, the instructional programs had a reputation for being dull because most were sequences of text and question formats. But today, with the vast increase in timesharing capabilities of computers, superior graphics, much improved instructional software, and the capability of linking your desktop computer into an information or educational network, there is an unlimited potential for computer-assisted instruction.

You might consider inquiring into the availability of computer-assisted instruction in your needed areas of employee training.

Vendors may have suggestions as may local universities or schools. One major example of the availability of online instruction is "The Electronic University" of the TeleLearning Corporation. It lists the availability of over 100 online courses in its current catalog, including programs leading toward bachelor's and master's degrees. Along with these courses, a student can also obtain counseling services, access an electronic library, and participate in various special seminar series. Bear in mind, too, that students can "attend" a seminar at any time; all they need to do is "log on" to the service.

To avoid problems of impersonalness, students can consult individually by appointment with instructors as well as handle all of their registration and administrative inquiries via their personal computer connections. The Electronic University claims official credit recognition for many of its offerings. For further information, write or call:

TeleLearning Systems, Inc.
5050 Beach Street
San Francisco, CA 94133
(800/225-3276)

Televised Instructional Services

If you are working at TRW, Hughes, or 34 other companies in the greater Los Angeles area, you can easily enroll in one or several of a dozen engineering and business courses offered each semester over the University of Southern California's Instructional Television Fixed Service System. You need never leave your business premises to enroll in a class because they are broadcast in audio and video form to a classroom located within your corporate environment. This classroom is much like any other except the instructor appears on a video screen, and if you wish to talk back to him or her, you "raise your hand" by pressing a button, then you speak into a desktop microphone. At the originating end of the system are several classrooms housed at the University of Southern California that are like any other, except for the presence of several small remote-controlled television cameras and a microphone that "captures" the day's lecture for transmission to the remote classrooms.

This brand of instructional television, technically called "ITFS" (Instructional Television Fixed Service), is not flashy or Hollywoodish (in fact, it can be a bit dull). It is a basic video and audio documentation of classroom proceedings for the USC Instructional Television Network. To save costs on remote facilities, feedback is audio only.

What are some of the advantages and disadvantages of ITFS Telelearning? In a study conducted by our former USC colleagues, one advantage consistently cited by students is that they probably would not have taken the course or pursued a degree program had the materials not been available for them on site in their companies. Distance from the university, schedule, and cost of transportation are typically cited as reasons for favoring the ITFS version. As for the success of learning in this environment, studies have indicated that receiving instruction at a remote site results in an equal amount of learning, comparable grades, and as high a motivation as attending regular university classrooms. In fact, on the positive side it has been the observation that students at remote class sites are sometimes more businesslike or serious about their work because it is integrated in a workday, as compared with a typical university student. An especially positive offering are the noon-hour, noncredit "Employee Development Programs," typically sponsored by co-operating companies.

On the negative side, the most frequent criticism is that there is little opportunity for classroom interaction in the ITFS environment. Although it is possible for students to ask questions over the audio feedback link of the system, the number of questions has to be limited when there are several remote classrooms involved, and students do not seem as inclined to ask questions as in live classrooms. But the interaction among students seems to be the more important factor here. ITFS simply does not allow students, except in their remote classrooms, to interact with one another. (In some cases, supervisors of remote classrooms have added extra time for class interaction.) A second and more subtle criticism is that in a society that prides itself in openness and spontaneity, the feeling that one must pay attention to a video display for 50 minutes in order to take a university class has felt less "pleasant" or "comfortable" than a "live" counterpart. Nonetheless, ITFS instruction has benefited literally thousands of students. You can adapt the ITFS instructional program to your specific needs by adding in-house sessions. In that way, not only do you train staff for specific tasks but you also overcome some of the program's lack of classroom student interaction.

Although ITFS programming is available at a limited number of universities (e.g., Stanford, Illinois Institute of Technology, and University of Maryland), there are at least three dozen universities that offer engineering, managerial, or technical education via special television or videotape services. If you are interested in obtaining such services, we suggest you contact your local university (business or engineering school, or continuing or extension education programs), write to the National Academy of Engineering in Washington D.C., the Corporation for Public Broadcasting (also in Washington), or call your local public broadcasting station.

Many firms in the technical training business have recognized the value of training with video and offer entire courses on videotape. Although they may be expensive (in the $5000 to $7000 range for a 30 hour course), they become your property and can be used to train new staff as they join your department or firm. As a manager you may find true bargains for your staff's continuing education through televised or videotape programs. And you might find something to benefit you, too.

A leader in the use of video for technical training is:

Integrated Computer Systems
5800 Hannum Avenue
P.O. Box 3614
Culver City, CA 90231-3614
(call 800/421-8166;
800/352-8251 in California)

Electronic Bulletin Boards

In Chapter 7, we described the use of "electronic bulletin boards" in organizational settings. For the price of a personal computer and peripherals (including a modem), you can establish a computer-based message and information service operating out of your own organization. Among the innovative uses we have observed for these "boards" are training and trouble-shooting services for new equipment implementation. For example, if new telecommunications software has been installed for exchanging data between micros and mainframes, a "board" could include a suggested tutorial to augment training manuals. The board could constantly be updated to circulate tips contributed by experienced users. As in the example described in Chapter 7, users could request trouble-shooting advice that could be answered several times per day by the individual in charge of training or implementation. Especially frequent problems could be answered by posting "bulletins."

A FINAL CAUTION

A final warning is that training is unfortunately deemphasized in many modern telecommunications implementations. Equipment and software vendors tend to underestimate the complexity of their products, stressing that their superiority includes less need for training (often not the case). Also, technical and other specialist personnel, both in the vendor's company and your organization, may underestimate training needs for nontechnical employees. Finally, new equipment budgeting traditionally underestimates training costs, especially hidden costs of employee time, travel, or time lost on the job itself.

On the other hand, remember that:

Modern concepts of office productivity are highly *human* oriented, meaning that it is the individual's contribution as enhanced by the technology that contributes to productivity, not just the technology itself.

Training is your key to this extra edge on productivity.

Telecommunications (teletraining) can help you solve your training challenge.

You should request that vendors offer you these critical services or give you advice for obtaining them. If they tend to downplay your training needs, look out; they are not fulfilling their responsibilities to you.

PART FOUR

GETTING YOUR EDGE
ON THE FUTURE

18
SIX STEPS TO BETTER MANAGEMENT WITH THE NEW TELECOMMUNICATIONS

TELECOMMUNICATIONS IS A STRATEGIC INVESTMENT

Telecommunications is a major resource of modern business. A McGraw-Hill study found that more than 15 percent of the senior executives of major U.S. firms viewed telecommunications as a priority investment for their future growth. Another 30 percent saw telecommunications as an investment necessary for the continued growth of their firms.

An executive of a major financial firm says that "to remain competitive we need to be innovative and cost effective in our use of telecommunications . . . . Telecommunications is a key to our future."

An executive of a large merchandising firm says that:

> Telecommunications investments are considered a part of our strategic plan. They provide the necessary support and services we need to move quickly in the marketplace. Telecommunications is a mandatory investment based on our need to move information rapidly and to stay competitive in a highly segmented market.

An executive of a computer consulting and software development firm says that "telecommunications is a critical component in the strategic and long term planning for corporate systems, services, and new products."

SIX STEPS TO BETTER MANAGEMENT

Telecommunications enables you to:

1. Get the right information you need at the right time. Information overload is the wrong information at the wrong time.
2. Reduce the high cost of labor. In today's information intensive business environment the workers you need the most, the *information workers,* are the most expensive workers. The new telecommunications reduces the cost of this labor.
3. Manage your money better. In an economy plagued by periodic bouts of inflation, efficient money management is the key to having the money you need to grow ahead of the competition.
4. Increase your span of management control. Firms that do not grow are candidates for takeover. You must expand your firm's capacity for business without excessively increasing your management and coordination requirements. The new telecommunications networks will help you to coordinate your organization, leaving management and planning to you and your key staff.
5. Get closer to your market. The closer you are to your market the faster you can respond to new market needs.
6. Develop new products and services, even new businesses. *USA TODAY* would not exist were it not for the new telecommunications.

THE RIGHT INFORMATION AT THE RIGHT TIME

The new telecommunications provides highly interactive communications for interpersonal message exchange, corporate information, and accessing outside databases. Furthermore, unlike in the past when you were essentially at the mercy of the telecommunications providers who set up the network for you, you can arrange and control your own network. Intelligent networks are software controlled, either from your telephone or from the PBX in your office. In this way you can perform your teleresearch, accessing information sources, and communicating simultaneously with the newly developed integrated voice/data terminals. While you search a database, you can teleconference on the same network, indeed, with the same terminal, and cross-check the data you are acquiring with your staff and consultants.

The new telecommunications allows for rapid low cost access to the information you need when you need it, no longer leaving you with the frustrations of too much of the wrong information. Information can be in the form you need in order to make your decisions. Multiple varieties of "what if" simulations can be on your terminal at your call, in your car, on the job, at home, and in your office.

Management is an information intensive activity. The new telecommunications provides you with the most important tools you need to manage effectively and competitively. You want immediate access of carefully selected information in the form that suits your decision-making style.

REDUCE LABOR COSTS

In an increasingly segmented marketplace, information is the key to staying ahead of the competition. People who can deal with that information are especially valuable and increasingly expensive. Information workers—researchers, data analysts, writers, secretaries, and clerks—are high cost workers, yet telecommunications can enhance their efforts.

The information technologies on networks made intelligent by the new telecommunications are your key to cost containment through office automation. Telecommunications enables you to share costly information processing power and to distribute this power where you need it most.

Software controlled intelligent telephones in the smaller offices enable you to allocate your telecommunications dollars to those tasks and people whose value to you are greatest. For the larger firm or office, you can choose between the carrier's Centrex services or your own PBX, again controlling the allocation of telecommunications resources and information resources in ways that enable you to reduce labor costs. Local area networks and voice/data PBXs offer the larger firms maximum allocation control to telecommunications costs across voice, video, image, and data communications as well as among widely dispersed work stations.

The new telecommunications enables you to redesign your information work, from a piecework office to a continuous process office. Tasks can be eliminated as multipurpose work stations can perform voice and data functions, electronic filing and mailing, and facsimile distribution.

Rethink your information tasks in the light of what telecommunications can do for you and you will significantly reduce information labor costs.

MANAGE YOUR MONEY BETTER

Citicorp's Walter Wriston is fond of saying that information about money is more valuable than money itself. You need more than bottom line figures about your money, you need to know what these figures mean.

Over the long term you will be managing in an inflationary economy. In this economy there are no "little" mistakes in cash management. One poor cash management decision, perhaps made without the right (often meaning the "latest") information, can lose you more money in a week than you can make up in 6 months of sales. The meaning behind the figures is the information you need to make the best decisions about how to manage your money.

Banks know this and are developing a wide range of cash management products and services to enable you to keep track of your money. Because money is information and information about money is money and more, these products and services are available on telecommunications networks.

The old saw that "time is money" is truer today than ever before; the longer a cash management error goes uncorrected, the more damaging it will be. Hence it is absolutely necessary that you have the telecommunications with which to access these cash management assists whenever you need to and from wherever you may be.

Your firm's or department's financial data and information should also be "on the network," appropriately protected from peering unauthorized eyes. The new telecommunications enables you to access both your firm's financial databases as well as the bank's products with which you can evaluate your cash positions and test alternative financial strategies. All of this can be done "on-line" via your personal computer linked to the telephone network, or even from an automobile via cellular mobile telephone.

There need no longer be any "little" mistakes in financial management.

INCREASE YOUR SPAN OF ORGANIZATIONAL CONTROL

General Motors did not purchase Electronic Data Systems (EDS) to get into the insurance business. General Motors purchased EDS to take advantage of the information and telecommunications technology for managing more with less.

The art of good management is to a great degree the art of communicating. The best thought out plans and programs of the brightest managers will go nowhere unless these plans can be communicated for your staff to implement. The best manager will know how to make the most effective use of all of the communications media available, from the "plain old telephone" to the computer, from the printed page delivered by mail to the facsimile transmitted by satellite across the nation, from "pressing the flesh" in a face-to-face conversation to a video conference with the Board.

The new telecommunications enables you to reach more people simultaneously and at lower cost than ever before possible. And you can delay your messages in order to reach staff in other time zones or if you feel that a timely delay will suit your strategic objectives. Modern telecommunications enables you to reach across space with teleconferences or to leap across time by means of store-and-forward telemail. This increases your management power and your executive reach with the important consequence that you may need fewer managers. The new telecommunications flattens the management hierarchy. Consider the comment by a major Los Angeles firm that reported:

> We eliminated an entire management level when we installed voice and data communications capability between headquarters and our remote sales and services offices. We found that our intelligent network can do the coordination our scheduling managers used to do. Now they can do what we hired them to do—that is, manage.

Executives who learn how to manage with the new telecommunications will find that they can decentralize responsibility without losing control. Furthermore, they can manage and coordinate many more dispersed activities with little or no increase in labor costs. Strategic investments in telecommunications are an important key to market power and corporate expansion with cost containment.

GET CLOSER TO YOUR MARKET

Success in the marketplace requires that you be an expert on your customers' needs. Clients want services and products designed to meet their special needs. If you do not respond to these needs, even if they are only hints, you lose out to the firm that has tapped this rapidly changing customer information, understood what it meant, and acted on it.

Telemarketing is a powerful tool not only because it links you to the customers quickly and often but because telemarketing enables you to listen to the marketplace and respond rapidly to the needs expressed.

Electronic catalog sales via the mass media and, even more so, cable television allow you to be in closer touch with your marketplace. The high office costs of handling direct mail operations are significantly reduced by automation in the office, by reorganizing your office to take advantage of the capabilities of multifunction equipment, such as communicating word processors for electronic mail, facsimile distribution systems, and electronic storage. Telecommunications is the key to coordinating these important applications. Local area networks and intelligent telephones can greatly reduce office costs while bringing you closer to your marketplace.

Examples abound of firms that are using telecommunications to reach out and stay in constant touch with their markets. General Electric provides a 24-hour service center via 800 long distance lines. The company can not only respond more rapidly to complaints and service requests but can monitor their product use in the marketplace and learn early about competition.

Xerox implemented a "Field Work Support System" on a telecommunications network to provide better and more cost effective service to its worldwide customer base of office equipment. Calls are placed to a support office where details of the client's equipment are kept in a computerized database. While the client is describing his or her problems, the file is called up and checked against the information provided. Often the diagnosis can take place on the telephone and if the problem is not solved, the field representative is dispatched well prepared for the repair job.

With new technologies, calls can be routed to your telecommuting employees who may be working from their homes, in satellite offices, or on the road. Savings in time and travel costs can be considerable.

Telecommunications that moves you closer to your client improves client satisfaction through faster and higher quality responses with fewer wasted visits because you did not have the right information before meeting with your client. Valuable experts and consultants are used much more productively if you are in close and constant touch with the people they are to service.

CREATE NEW SERVICES, PRODUCTS, AND BUSINESSES

"Merrill Lynch Cash Management Account" would not be on the market today were it not for the new telecommunications. General Motors would not be able to produce the low cost, highly competitive Saturn were it not for the new manufacturing processes made possible by telecommunications. American Hospital Supply (AHS) developed an order entry system that uses 4000 interconnected terminals throughout the nation, giving them more direct access to their customers and thereby creating a highly protective barrier to competition. Not only do the customers have direct access to the AHS order and distribution process, they are sold software products for performing inventory control. AHS now generates more orders for their traditional products and they have new services to sell as well.

Information technology and telecommunications can restructure internal manufacturing and office operations in ways that enable firms to offer entirely new products in the marketplace as well as lower the costs of their existing products. Expert systems interconnected by local area networks allow specialty computer manufacturers to meet the custom needs of their customers more rapidly and at lower cost than do the competitors.

You can take a traditional product sales operation and alter the competitive marketplace by linking yourself closer to that marketplace. And while doing this you can uncover new services to offer and increase your revenue.

FIVE QUESTIONS YOU MUST ANSWER TO MAKE TELECOMMUNICATIONS A STRATEGIC RESOURCE FOR YOUR BUSINESS

You must think of information technology and especially telecommunications strategically. Ask these five important questions as you plan your telecommunications investments.

1. How can you use the technology to make significant changes in the way you do business so that you can gain a competitive advantage?
2. How can information technology improve your sensitivity to the marketplace?
3. How can you make internal improvements in how your department or firm carries out their activities, improvements that will increase staff and managerial effectiveness, as well as overall productivity?
4. What new products and services can you offer that information technology and telecommunications make possible?
5. How can you manage more effectively with information technology and telecommunications?

REFERENCES

Bell, D. 1976. *The coming of post industrial society: A venture in social forecasting*. New York: Basic Books, Harper.

Cherry, C. 1980. *On human communication: A review, a survey, and a criticism;* 3rd ed. Cambridge, MA: MIT Press.

Dertouzes, M. L., and J. Moses. 1980. *The computer age: A twenty year view*. Cambridge, MA: MIT Press.

Dordick, H. S. 1986. *Understanding modern telecommunications*, New York: McGraw-Hill.

Dordick, H. S. *Information policy as related to EFTS in the financial marketplace*. Washington, D. C.: U.S. Government Printing Office. June 1980.

Dordick, H. S., H. G. Bradley, and B. Nanus. 1981. *The emerging network marketplace*. Norwood, NY: Ablex.

Drucker, P. F. 1982. *The changing world of the executive*. New York: Times Books.

Drucker, P. F. 1980. *Managing in turbulent times*. New York: Harper & Row.

Drucker, P. F. 1969. *The age of discontinuity: Managing in turbulent times*. New York: Harper & Row.

EFT in the United States: Policy Recommendations and the Public Interest. Washington D. C.: U.S. Government Printing Office, 1977.

Forester, T. (ed.) 1981. *The microelectronics revolution*. Cambridge, MA: MIT Press.

Goldmark, P. C. 1972. Tomorrow we will communicate to our jobs. *The Futurist 6* (2) April: 35–42.

Griesinger, F.K. 1974. *How to cut costs and improve service of your telephone telex, TWX, and other telecommunications*. New York: McGraw-Hill.

Howitt, D. and I. W. Marvin. 1984. *Inc. magazines' databasics*. New York: Garland.

Johansen, R. 1984. *Teleconferencing and beyond*. New York: McGraw-Hill.

Martin, J. 1977. *Telecommunications and the computer*, 2nd ed. Englewood Cliffs, NJ: Prentice-Hall.

Meadows, C. T., and A. S. Tedesco. 1985. *Telecommunications for management*. New York: McGraw-Hill.

Mintzberg, H. 1973. *The nature of managerial work.* New York: Harper & Row.

Nilles, J. M., F. R. Carlson, Jr., P. Gray, and G. J. Hannemann. 1976. *The telecommunication-transportation tradeoff: Options for tomorrow.* New York: Wiley-Interscience.

Porat, M. U. *The Information Economy.* (OT Special Publication 77-12(1)). Washington, D. C.: U.S. Dept. of Commerce, May 1977.

Revolution in telecommunications is broader then electronic funds transfer. *American Banker,* December 29, 1978, 5.

Rice, R., and Associates. 1984. *The new media.* Beverly Hills: Sage.

Servan-Schreiber. J. J. 1981. *The world challenge.* New York: Simon & Schuster.

Singleton, L. A. 1983. *Telecommunications in the information age.* Cambridge, MA: Ballinger.

Smith, D. 1981. Info City. *New York* (February 9): 24–29.

Strassmann, P. 1985. *Information payoff.* New York: Free Press.

Toffler, A. 1980. *The third wave.* New York: Morrow.

Williams, F. 1983. *The communications revolution.* New York: New American Library.

Williams, F., and H. S. Dordick 1983. *The executive's guide to information technology.* New York: Wiley.

GLOSSARY

ACCESS CHANNEL. A cable television channel dedicated to public use often with provisions for the general public to originate its own programs, but sometimes only for governmental or educational purposes.

ACOUSTIC MODEM. An instrument (modem) for connecting your computer to the telephone network via the speaker and receiver parts of your telephone handset (as opposed to a direct wire modem).

AM. Amplitude Modulation (see modulation).

ANALOG. Representations that bear some physical relationship to the original quantity: usually electrical voltage, frequency, resistance, or mechanical translation or rotation.

ANSWER. A setting on a modem that sets you up to receive an incoming call from a computer (see originate).

ANTENNA. A device used to collect and/or radiate radio energy.

ARTIFICIAL INTELLIGENCE. Computer programs that perform functions, often by imitation, usually associated with human reasoning and learning.

ASCII. (pronounced ask-ee). American Standard Code for Information Interchange. The binary transmission code used by most teletypewriters and display terminals.

AUTOANSWER. Modems that will answer the telephone for you and receive incoming computer communications.

AUTODIAL.   Modems or communications software that will dial or redial numbers stored in their memory.

BAND.   A range of radio frequencies within prescribed limits of the radio frequency spectrum.

BANDWIDTH.   The width of an electrical transmission path or circuit, in terms of the range of frequencies it can pass; a measure of the volume of communications traffic that the channel can carry. A voice channel typically has a bandwidth of 4000 cycles per second; a TV channel requires about 6.5 MHz.

BASEBAND.   An information or message signal whose content extends from a frequency near dc to some finite value. For voice, baseband extends from 300 hertz (Hz) to 3400 Hz. Video baseband is from 50 Hz to 4.2 MHz (NTSC standard).

BAUD.   Bits per second (bps) in a binary (two-state) telecommunications transmission. After Emile Baudot, the inventor of the asynchronous telegraph printer.

BELL-COMPATIBLE.   Essentially this means that a modem conforms to the standards of the Bell Telephone System.

BINARY.   A numbering system having only digits, typically 0 and 1.

BIT.   Binary digit. The smallest part of information with values or states of 0 or 1, or yes or no. In electrical communication system, a bit can be represented by the presence or absence of a pulse.

BRANCH.   This refers to alternatives on selection menus in a database information service or among alternative parts of a computer program.

BROADBAND CARRIERS.   The term to describe high capacity transmission systems used to carry large blocks of, for instance, telephone channels or one or more video channels. Such broadband systems may be provided by coaxial cables and repeated amplifiers or microwave radio systems.

BROADBAND COMMUNICATION.   A communications system with a bandwidth greater than voiceband. Cable is a broadband communication system with a bandwidth usually from 5 MHz to 450 MHz.

BUFFER.   A machine or other device to be inserted between other machines or devices to match systems or speeds, prevent unwanted interaction, or delay the rate of information flow.

BULLETIN BOARD (ELECTRONIC). A contemporary service whereby individuals or organizations set up computers and communications equipment so as to maintain message files for a group of users.

BYTE. A group of bits processed or operating together. Bytes are often an 8-bit group, but 16-bit and 32-bit bytes are not uncommon.

CABLE TELEVISION. The use of a broadband cable (coaxial cable or optical fiber) to deliver video signals directly to television sets in contrast to over-the-air transmissions. Current systems may have the capability of receiving data inputs from the viewer and of transmitting video signals in two directions, permitting pay services and video conferencing from selected locations.

CAD. Computer Aided Design. Techniques that use computers to help design machinery and electronic components.

CAI. Computer Assisted Instruction.

CAM. Computer Aided Manufacturing.

CARRIER SIGNAL. The tone that you hear when you manually dial into a computer network.

CATHODE RAY TUBE. Called CRT, this is the display unit or screen of your computer.

CCITT. Consultative Committee for International Telephone and Telegraphs, an arm of the International Telecommunications Union (ITU), which establishes voluntary standards for telephone and telegraph interconnection.

CENTRAL OFFICE. The local switch for a telephone system, sometimes referred to as a wire center.

CHANNEL. A segment of bandwidth that may be used to establish a communications link. A television channel has a bandwidth of 6 MHz, a voice channel about 4000 Hz.

CHIP. A single device made up of transistors, diodes, and other components, interconnected by chemical process and forming the basic component of microprocessors.

CIRCUIT SWITCHING. The process by which a physical interconnection is made between two circuits or channels.

COAXIAL CABLE. A metal cable consisting of a conductor surrounded by another conductor in the form of a tube that can carry broadband signals by guiding high-frequency electromagnetic radiation.

CODE. Giving a computer instructions in computer readable language, as in coding a program.

COMMON CARRIER. An organization licensed by the Federal Communications Commission (FCC) and/or by various state public utility commissions to supply communications services to all users at established and stated prices.

COMMUNICATIONS BOARD (PORT). Special circuitry that you may need to purchase in order for your communicator to be able to communicate.

COMMUNICATIONS SETTINGS. Whatever is necessary for two computers to use the same communication system; often called protocol.

COMPILER. An automatic computer coding system that generates and assembles a program from instructions prepared by equipment manufacturers or software companies.

COMPUTER WORD. A string of characters or binary numbers considered as one unit and stored at a single computer address or location.

COMSAT. Communications Satellite Corporation. A private corporation authorized by the Communications Satellite Act of 1962 to represent the United States in international satellite communications and to operate domestic and international satellites.

CONNECT TIME. Typically this is the amount of time that you are linked to a computer database service; it is the basis for calculating your fees.

CP/M. Control program for microprocessor. A microcomputer operating system that is sometimes recognized as a standard.

CPU. The central processing unit of a computer.

CRT. See cathode ray tube.

CURSOR. This is whatever mark or indicator is on your computer screen to tell your position on that screen. For example, if you start typing, each item of text will appear where the cursor has been.

DATABASE. Information or files stored in a computer for subsequent retrieval and use. Many of the services obtained from information utilities actually involve accessing large databases.

DCE. Data communications equipment, computer components that are designed to communicate directly to data terminal equipment. (See DTE.)

DEDICATED LINES. Telephone lines leased for a specific term between specific points on a network, usually to provide certain special services not otherwise available on the public watched network.

DEMODULATE. A process in which information is recovered from a carrier.

DIGITAL. A function that operates in discrete steps as contrasted to a continuous or analog function. Digital computers manipulate numbers encoded into binary (on-off) forms, while analog computers sum continuously varying forms. Digital communication is the transmission of information using discontinuous, discrete electrical or electromagnetic signals that change in frequency, polarity, or amplitude. Analog intelligence may be encoded for transmission on digital communication systems (see pulse code modulation).

DIRECT BROADCAST SATELLITE (DBS). A satellite system designed with sufficient power so that inexpensive earth stations can be used for direct residential or community reception, thus reducing the need for local loop by allowing use of a receiving antennae with a diameter that is less than one meter.

DISK. A magnetized surface capable of storing binary information.

DISK OPERATING SYSTEM. An operating program that instructs the computer how to store and retrieve information from a disk. (See CP/M, MS/DOS.)

DOS. See disk operating system.

DOT MATRIX. A computer-driven printer that prints symbols with a matrix of small pins (as distinguished from letter quality).

DOWNLINK. An antenna designed to receive signals from a communications satellite (see uplink).

DOWNLOAD. To receive information from another computer and store it into your computer memory or disk files.

DTE. Data terminal equipment, designates a communications configuration designed to communicate to data communications equipment. Often a computer is DTE whereas a modem is DCE. If you are linking together two DTE or DCE components, you will need a crossover cable.

DUMB TERMINAL.   See terminal.

DUPLEX.   The condition when information can flow two ways simultaneously in a communication link. This condition is often called full duplex as contrasted with one-way communications or half duplex. For most of your computer communication services, you will want a full duplex condition.

EARTH STATION.   A communication station on the surface of the earth used to communicate with a satellite. (Also TVRO, television receive only earth station.)

ELECTRONIC MAIL.   The delivery of correspondence, including graphics, by electronic means, usually by the interconnection of computers, word processors, or facsimile equipment.

ENCRYPTION.   To change from a plain text to an encoded form requiring sophisticated techniques for decoding. Digital information can be encrypted directly with computer software.

ESS.   Electronic switching system. The Bell System designation for their stored program control switching machines.

FAX.   Facsimile. A system for the transmission of images. It is a black and white reproduction of a document or picture transmitted over a telephone or other transmission system.

FCC.   Federal Communications Commission. A board of five members (commissioners) appointed by the president and confirmed by the Senate under the provision of the Communications Act of 1934. The FCC has the power to regulate interstate communications.

FILE (COMPUTER).   Information stored in a computer is typically referred to as a file. Large files that contain information for retrieval are typically called databases.

FINAL MILE.   The communications systems required to get from the earth station to where the information or program is to be received and used. Terrestrial broadcasting from local stations and/or cable television systems provide the final mile for today's satellite networks.

FIRMWARE.   Instructions for operation of computer or communications equipment embedded in the electrical design of a microchip.

FLOPPY DISK. The plastic disk used to store information or programs (see disk).

FM. Frequency modulation (see modulation).

FREE TEXT SEARCH. The capability for scanning through text files in order to locate certain specified words (key words).

FREQUENCY. The number of recurrences of a phenomenon during a specified period of time. Electrical frequency is expressed in hertz, equivalent to cycles per second.

FREQUENCY SPECTRUM. A term describing a range of frequencies of electromagnetic waves in radio terms; the range of frequencies useful for radio communication, from about 10 Hz to 3000 GHz.

FULL DUPLEX. See duplex.

GATEWAY. The ability of one information service to transfer you to another one, as when you go from Dow Jones/News Retrieval to MCI Mail.

GEOSTATIONARY SATELLITE. A satellite, with a circular orbit 22,400 miles in space, which lies in the satellite plane of the Earth's equator and which turns about the polar axis of the Earth in the same direction and with the same period as that of the Earth's rotation. Thus, the satellite is stationary when viewed from the Earth.

GIGAHERTZ (GHz). Billion cycles per second.

HALF DUPLEX. Message flow is only one-way at a time. See duplex.

HANDSHAKING. Jargon for the electronic exchange of signals as one computer links with another.

HARD COPY. See printout.

HARDWARE. The electrical and mechanical equipment used in telecommunications and computer systems (see software; firmware).

HARD WIRE MODEM. Or direct modem; as contrasted with an acoustic modem, this equipment plugs directly into a telephone jack.

HEADEND. The electronic control center of the cable television system where weaving signals are amplified, filtered, or converted as necessary. The headend is usually located at or near the antenna site.

HERTZ (Hz). The frequency of an electric or electromagnetic wave in cycles per second, named after Heinrich Hertz who detected such waves in 1883.

HOST. The main computer or computer system that is supporting a group of users.

IEEE. Institute of Electrical and Electronic Engineers. A professional society.

INFORMATION UTILITY. A term increasingly used to refer to services that offer a wide variety of information, communications, and computing services to subscribers; examples are The Source, CompuServe, or Dow Jones News/Retrieval.

INTERFACE. The equipment programs or procedures that enable components of a computer system or two computers to exchange information or interact.

INSTITUTIONAL LOOP. A separate cable for a CATV system designed to serve public institutions or businesses usually with two-way video and data services.

INTERFACE. Devices that operate at a common boundary of adjacent components or systems and that enable these components or systems to interchange information.

I/O-INPUT-OUTPUT. The equipment or processes that transmit data into or out of a computer's central processing unit.

K. 1024 bytes of information, or roughly the same number of symbols, or digits.

KILOHERTZ (KHz). Thousand cycles per second.

LAN. See local area network.

LASER. Light amplification by simulated emission of radiation. An intense beam that can be modulated for communications.

LETTER QUALITY. Printers that produce text similar to that produced by a high quality typewriter, as often contrasted with a dot matrix printer.

LOCAL AREA NETWORK (LAN). A special linkage of computers or other communications devices into their own network for use by an individual or organization. Local area networks are part of the modern trend of office communication systems.

LOOP. The wire pair that extends from a telephone central office to a telephone instrument. The coaxial cable in a broadband or CATV system that passes by each building or residence on a street and connects with the trunk cable at a neighborhood node is often called the Subscriber Loop.

LSI. Large-scale integration. Single integrated circuits that contain more than 100 logic circuits on one microchip. (see VLSI)

MAINFRAME. The base or main part of a large computer, as contrasted with mini- or microcomputers. Usually refers to the actual processing unit.

MASS STORAGE. A device that can hold very large amounts of information cheaply with automated access on demand.

MEGAHERTZ (MHz). Million cycles per second.

MEMORY. One of the basic components of a central processing unit (CPU). It stores information for future use.

MENU (COMPUTER). A list of alternatives given to you from which you select to obtain the options you seek. Most major information utilities have an entire hierarchy or sequence of menus so that by going from one menu to another you can work your way to the desired program or service.

MICROCHIP. An electronic circuit with multiple solid-state devices engraved through photolithographic or microbeam processes on one substrate (see microcomputer; microprocessor).

MICROCOMPUTER. A set of microchips that can perform all of the functions of a digital stored-program computer. (See microprocessor.)

MICROPROCESSOR. A microchip that performs the logic functions of a digital computer.

MICROSECOND. One millionth of a second.

MICROWAVE. The short wave lengths from 1 GHz to 30 GHz used for radio, television, and satellite systems.

MILLISECOND. One thousandth of a second.

MINICOMPUTER. In general, a minicomputer is a stationary computer that has more computer power than a microcomputer but less than a large mainframe computer.

MODEM. Short for modulator-demodulator. The equipment that you use to link your computer to a telephone line.

MODULATION. A process of modifying the characteristics of a propagating signal, such as a carrier, so that it represents the instantaneous changes of another signal. The carrier wave can change its amplitude (AM), its frequency (FM), its phase, or its duration (pulse code modulation), or combinations of these.

MONITOR (VIDEO). Usually refers to the video screen on computer but has more technical meanings as well.

MOUSE. Refers to a simple device for moving a marker on a computer screen in order to give the computer commands.

MS/DOS. Microsoft Disk Operating System. An operating system for microcomputers made standard by wide use of IBM personal computers.

MULTIPLEXING. A process of combining two or more signals from separate sources into a single signal for sending on a transmission system from which the original signals may be recovered.

NANOSECOND. One billionth of a second.

NARROWBAND COMMUNICATION. A communication system capable of carrying only voice or relatively slow speed computer signals.

NETWORK. The circuits over which computers or other devices may be connected with one another, such as over the telephone network, or one can speak of computer networking.

NODE. A point at which terminals and other computer and telecommunications equipment are connected to the transmissions network.

OFF-LINE. Equipment not connected to a telecommunications system or an operating computer system.

ON-LINE. A device normally connected to a telecommunications or computing system.

OPERATING SYSTEM. Instructions for a microcomputer that permit it to run various programs and handle scheduling, control of printers, terminals, memory devices, and so forth. (See CP/M; MS/DOS.)

OPTICAL FIBER. A thin flexible glass fiber the size of a human hair which will transmit light waves capable of carrying large amounts of information.

ORBIT. The path of a satellite around the earth.

ORIGINATE. Sets a modem up to initiate computer communications link (see answer).

PBX. A private branch exchange which may or may not be automated. Also called PABX (private automatic branch exchange).

PACKET SWITCHING. A technique of switching digital signals with computers wherein the signal stream is broken into packets and reassembled in the correct sequence at the destination.

PARALLEL INTERFACE. Refers to a computer communications connection where the bits code for a symbol is sent simultaneously as contrasted with serial interface, where the symbols are sent in sequence.

PERIPHERALS. Units that operate in conjunction with a computer but are not a part of it, for example, printers, modems, or disk drive.

PERSONAL COMPUTER. A microcomputer that tends to be used more for business purposes than for games or recreation, but the distinction is not all that exact.

PORT. A place of communication signal entrance or exit to and from a computer.

PRINTOUT. Materials listed by your printer; sometimes called hard copy.

PROGRAM. A set of instructions arranged in proper sequence for directing a computer to perform desired operation.

PROTOCOL. A description of the requirements for enabling one computer to communicate with another.

PULSE CODE MODULATIONS (PCM). A technique by which a signal is sampled periodically, each sample quantitized, and transmitted as a signal binary code.

RAM. Random access memory. A RAM provides access to any storage or memory location point directly by means of vertical and horizontal coordinates. It is erasable and reusable.

READ. Literally means for your computer to read information either from storage in its own memory or from disk or tape.

RETURN KEY. A holdover from the carriage return of a typewriter keyboard, the return key is used to tell your computer to execute what it has received. It is sometimes called an enter or execute key.

ROBOTICS. The use of electronic control techniques, as programmed on microprocessors and microcomputers, to operate mechanical sensing and guidance mechanisms or robots in manufacturing and assembly processes.

ROM. Read only memory. A permanently stored memory which is read out and not altered in the operation.

RS232. An interface between a modem and associated data terminal equipment. It is standardized.

SCROLL. This typically refers to the vertical movement of the display or text on the computer screen. Occasionally instead of just receiving one screenful of information at a time, you will want the information to scroll continuously.

SIGN-ON.   Jargon for initiating your connection with an information service by providing your account designation and password; the same as log-on. Sign off refers to disconnecting from
a communications link, often the same as log-out.

SLOW-SCAN TELEVISION.   A technique of placing video signals on a
narrowband circuit, such as telephone lines, which results in a
picture changing every few seconds.

SOFTWARE.   The written instructions which direct a computer program. Any written material or script for use on a communications system or the program produced from the script. (See
hardware, firmware.)

SYSOP.   In computer jargon, systems operator, or the person who
operates a computer bulletin board or a conference or mail system.

SYSTEMS PROGRAM.   As contrasted with an applications program
which accomplishes specific tasks (e.g., word processing), this
supports the basic operating system of the computer, for example, in allocating memory storage and operating peripherals.

TARIFF.   The published rate for a service, equipment, or facility established by the communications common carrier.

TELECOMMUTING.   The use of computers and telecommunications
to enable people to work at home. More broadly, the substitution of telecommunications for transportation.

TELECONFERENCE.   The simultaneous visual and/or sound interconnection that allows individuals in two or more locations to
see and talk to one another in a long distance conference arrangement.

TELEMARKETING.   A method of marketing that emphasizes the creative use of the telephone and other telecommunications systems.

TELETEXT.   The generic name for a set of systems which transmit
alphanumeric and simple graphical information over the
broadcast (or one-way cable) signal, using spare line capacity
in the signal for display on a suitably modified TV receiver.

TELEX.   A dial-up telegraph service.

TERMINAL.   A point at which a communication can either leave or
enter a communications network.

TERMINAL EMULATOR. Use of a personal computer to act as a dumb terminal; this requires special software or firmware.

TIMESHARING. When a computer can support two or more users. The large computers used by the information utilities can accommodate many users simultaneously who are said to be timesharing on the system.

TRANSPONDER. The electronic circuit of a satellite that receives a signal from the transmitting earth station, amplifies it, and transmits it to the Earth at a different frequency.

TRUNK. A main cable that runs from the head end to a local node, then connects to the drop running to a home in a cable television system; a main circuit connected to local central offices with regional or intercity switches in telephone systems.

TWISTED PAIR. The term given to the two wires that connect local telephone circuits to the telephone central office.

UPLINK. The communications link from the transmitting Earth station to the satellite.

UPLOAD. To transfer information out of the memory or disk file of your computer to another computer.

USER FRIENDLY. A popular term that means that a computer, a program, or a system is easy to learn or easy to use.

VIDEO MONITOR. The visual display screen part of your computer.

VIDEOTEXT. The generic name for a computer system that transmits alphanumeric and simple graphics information over the ordinary telephone line for display on a video monitor.

VLSI. Very large scale integration. Single integrated circuits that contain more than 100,000 logic gates on one microchip (see LSI).

WATS. Wide area telephone service. A service offered by telephone companies in the United States that permits customers to make dial calls to telephones in a specific area for a flat monthly charge, or to receive calls collect at a flat monthly charge.

WRITE. In computer jargon this means to transfer a file to disk or tape or some storage medium.

A

A CHECKLIST FOR PLANNING NEW TELECOMMUNICATIONS

Use this handy checklist to write proposals for telecommunications investments, for preparing bid requests, for designing implementation procedures and schedules, and for evaluating your investments.

1. *Needs Assessment*
   1.1   *What type of needs assessment is best for you? (equipment or software update? organizational changes? new business? improve return on investment?)*
   1.2   *Who will be responsible for the needs assessment?*
   1.3   *Can you be compatible with existing information technology?*
   1.4   *What will implications be for further growth?*
   1.5   *Will you be changing the way you do business?*
   1.6   *What are the organizational implications?*
   1.7   *Will new business opportunities be created?*
   1.8   *Are there existing examples of the implementation?*
   1.9   *What is your implementation timetable?*
   1.10 *At which managerial level will responsibility be placed?*
   1.11 *Will managerial changes be involved?*
   1.12 *Are changes in corporate policy likely to be required?*
   1.13 *Have you designed an evaluation plan?*
   1.14 *What are your best telecommunications investments?*

2. Procurement

2.1   Who is in charge of procurement?

2.2   Who will write the specifications?

2.3   What is your financing plan?

2.4   What are the relative advantages of lease versus purchase?

2.5   What are your needs for training?

2.6   Are vendors readily available?

2.7   What are procedures for receiving and evaluating bids?

2.8   Is there a need for a special or a new procurement policy?

3. Implementation

3.1   Who is responsible for the implementation?

3.2   What is your realistic timetable?

3.3   How will training be integrated?

3.4   How will maintenance of your system be provided?

3.5   If new personnel are necessary, what is your recruitment plan?

3.6   What are your strategies for motivating use of the new technology?

3.7   Are you implementing any new cost-accounting procedures?

4. Evaluation

4.1   Who is in charge of evaluation?

4.2   What revisions are necessary in your original plan?

4.3   How and when are performance standards to be evaluated?

4.4   What is the plan for a cost review (including tariffs)?

4.5   Have you prioritized major problems to be surmounted?

4.6   Are more or different organization changes required?

4.7   What are the overall consequences for your place in the competitive marketplace?

4.8   Can you clearly identify the ''pay off''—that is, value-added?

4.9   What is your next innovation?

4.10   What are the implications for long-range planning?

APPENDIX
B

SUGGESTIONS FOR
MANAGING
THE USE OF VIDEO
DISPLAY TERMINALS

Consider these suggestions when designing work spaces, selecting furniture, or planning policy and work routines involving video display terminals (VDTs). Workers with eye strain or fatigue become inefficient and often inaccurate; also, morale problems can spread. Meet the VDT issues head on. Also, think about your own use of terminals; some of these suggestions will be valuable to your work on a terminal in your office, at home, or on the road.

1. *Preventing Eye Strain from Glare*
   1.1 *Guard against troublesome glare from windows, light sources, or lightly colored objects (including clothing) that can reflect in the screen.*

   1.2 *Check on the position of VDTs. It is not unusual for VDTs initially to be located where typewriters were; the two require different lighting conditions.*

   1.3 *Investigate purchase of matte surface or nonglare screens. Know that they may be slightly less satisfactory for detailed work and are sometimes more difficult to clean.*

   1.4 *Consider indirect overhead lighting.*

   1.5 *Use drapes or shades to reduce glare.*

   1.6 *Be prepared for glare problems with LED (''flat'') screens.*

2. *Anxiety About Radiation*

   2.1 *There is no major evidence that the leading brands of VDTs are a radiation hazard; however, there is no way to know of very-long-range effects, especially on unborn children.*

   2.2 *Precautions include having measures taken to assure that radiation levels are within safe standards. Have a consultant advise you on such measures and standards.*

   2.3 *Meet the problem head-on with your workers; inform them of what is known and thereby discourage rumors.*

3. *Screen Resolution and Color; Work Position*

   3.1 *Fit the screen resolution to the job; for example, proofreading is more demanding than general text input, or design graphics more critical than simple, numerical figures.*

   3.2 *Consider your alternatives for screen display—for example, black text on white background, amber versus green, and so on. Have users select the screen type.*

   3.3 *Consider color, especially where distinctions are relevant to the work material (order forms, design graphics). Color is generally less taxing on the eyes and more pleasant to the user (although studies have often indicated that color is not critical to work efficiency).*

   3.4 *Keep reference work (e.g., material to be copied) in a well lighted position and approximately the same distance from the operator as is the VDT screen. (Some eye problems are not from the VDT screen but from other sources.)*

4. *Eyecare*

   4.1 *Encourage periodic eye examinations (even on-site as a company routine). Inform the ophthalmologist that work involves a VDT environment. Special glasses may benefit VDT work.*

   4.2 *Check with your ophthalmologist about special relaxing techniques or exercises workers can use to avoid eye strain.*

   4.3 *Set up procedures for regular breaks—for example, a few minutes each hour—away from the screen. Consider routines for alternating with non-VDT work.*

   4.4 *Encourage objective knowledge and a positive concern about eyecare among your employees.*

5. *Avoid Physical Fatigue*

 5.1 *Use chair and desk furniture designed for VDT work. Usually they are adjustable to suit different individuals. The center of the VDT screen is best about 20 degrees down from the viewer's straight-ahead eye level. Distance to the screen is best at about 15 to 20 inches, but can vary for the comfort of different individuals.*

 5.2 *Set up procedures where breaks are away from the desk, perhaps in a coffee room.*

6. *Avoid Mental Fatigue*

 6.1 *Because some VDT work can be highly intense mentally, it is important to set up work schedules so individuals can refresh themselves. A common recommendation is that a 15 minute alternate task break be given each hour if VDT use is intensive, or every 2 hours if use is moderate.*

 6.2 *Improper or insufficient training may have resulted in fatiguing work habits. Examine worker routines, and include the most efficient and comfortable in your training schedule.*

 6.3 *Encourage workers to discuss their work procedures with you. It may be possible to develop innovative schedules for work combinations that lessen the possibility of fatigue.*

Index